Alastair Ebenezer Buchan,
Lieutenant, Royal Scots Fusiliers
12th June 1894 – 9th April 1917

1. Alastair's formal photograph by Vandyk, London

John Buchan's Kid Brother

Alastair Ebenezer Buchan,
Lieutenant, Royal Scots Fusiliers
12th June 1894 – 9th April 1917

David Weekes

Lavender *Inprint*

First published as an abridged version in the
John Buchan Journal 2019
This edition enlarged and revised October 2022
Published by Lavender Inprint
235A Rotherhithe Street,
London, SE16 5XW

All communications should be addressed to
lavender.inprint@gmail.com

The Reverend Dr David Weekes (born 1934) asserts
the moral right to be the author of this publication

ISBN 979 - 8 – 6761860 - 2 - 9

The author has written a number of books since two were
published by Gupta in Mbarara in 1970. Other presently
available titles by the same author include:

The Origins of Lexham Gardens and Lee Abbey in London.
Leominster: Gracewing, 1996

What Sir William Fettes Really Meant
London: Lavender, 2010; available from publisher

ΧΡΙΣΤΟΣ ΝΙΚΗΣΕΙ On John Buchan's Grave. London:
Lavender, 2010

How Captain James set Churchill on the Path to Glory.
London: Lavender, 2010;
republished by Amazon online, 2020

Kilmany in Fife: *Glimpses of History.*
London: Lavender, 2013
available from Amazon online, 2018

Mbarara Genesis. London: Lavender, 2014
available from Amazon online, 2018

John Buchan, 1875-1940 (First Baron Tweedsmuir of Elsfield): Reassessing some Influences on, and Prejudices in his Practice of the Christian Faith.
University of St Andrews online, 2017

John Buchan's Faith Experienced in His Life. London: Lavender, 2022.

In preparation:

"John Buchan's Faith and Issues in Some of His Prose"

"John Buchan: Essays in His Honour"

"Nkore Religion and Christianity"

*2. A soldier of the Royal Scots Fusiliers in 1916,
dressed as Alastair would have led them
into battle. From a water colour by
Lieut.-Col. A. G. Baird-Smith, RSF*

To the Memory of
all the subalterns who
"poured out the red sweet wine of youth"
and did not return
from the First World War,
and
especially to one.

"And those who would have been their sons, they gave"

(Rupert Brooke, "The Dead")

The Author

The Reverend Dr David Weekes was born in 1934. After graduating from Magdalene College, Cambridge, he taught and did Christian social work for a few years before training to be ordained by the Bishop of Chester in 1964 and 1965. Having served for four years as a curate in the Cheshire environs of Manchester he went to Uganda, supported by the Church Missionary Society, on a British Government aid scheme. He taught A level English as Chaplain of Ntare School, Mbarara, coupled with an honorary responsibility on Sundays for the English-speaking congregation in the local Anglican cathedral. This was under Bishop Kosiya Shalita, and as the only non-African clergyman in the diocese of Ankole. He returned to spend two decades teaching as Chaplain of Fettes College in Edinburgh. Thereafter he was Warden and Chaplain of Lee Abbey International Students' Club in Kensington which provides for up to two hundred students from many nations. Married with three children, now nine grandchildren, and a great-grandson, he retired to his old home in the north of Fife, where he is a part-time freelance writer. Having published books about the historical background in the places where he has served and rural Fife, together with a monograph about young Churchill, he has been intrigued by John Buchan since boyhood, inspired through his father's interest. A member of The John Buchan Society since 1980, this is the third book that he has written about that family. Throughout there has been a particular concern to emphasise the sometimes much neglected bed-rock foundation governing their lives and inspiring their actions, a life-long and deeply committed Christian faith. What action he has seen has been as a child in London throughout the War, as a subaltern at Tel-el-Kebir helping to guard the Suez Canal against insurgency, and as an Education Officer well into

Idi Amin's terrifyingly brutal usurpation of power in Uganda, mainly affecting the tyrant's own people, and including the killing of pupils. Among his hobbies has been the building of rugged boundary walls round his home from old stone largely found on site, and influenced perhaps by living in an ancient listed building composed of such material, once thatched but long since pan-tiled from across the German Ocean. He is a Fellow of the Royal Historical Society and of the Society of Antiquaries of Scotland. His doctorate was on John Buchan, hence this curiosity about the unsung kid brother.

ACKNOWLEGEMENTS

I am grateful to Ursula Buchan (the Honourable Mrs Charles Wide) and Dr Michael Redley for their help, and encouraging me to undertake this study. Ursula has kindly interpreted the calligraphy of some of her forebears.

All within the family have been supportive. My wife, Jean, has been ever lovingly patient; of my two sons, Dr Richard, sometime a Major in the R.A.M.C., has been my inspiration about the work of army doctors, while the Reverend Robin made helpful suggestions, and read some parts of the draft. My daughter, Catriona, contributed much latterly. My grandson, Alistair, was a great assistance in placing the photographs and in other matters of layout and production, as was his father, Professor Saleem Bhatti. My daughter-in-law, Dr Ursula has paced me in writing another book of her own and encouraged me.

Edward Armstrong, of the Universities of Sydney and St Andrews, has kindly read my draft and prepared it for publication. I have found so often that the detailed works of supererogation by archivists and librarians have continued to impress and enlighten me. I hope to have named them in the footnotes. They are a race apart, and to them much gratitude is due.

At first I was especially baffled about any details of the lives of Alastair's fellow officers in the 6/7th Royal Scots Fusiliers, Skeil, Colonel Gordon, and Major Smith, and failed to make contact with the Museum of that regiment. The first two eventually fell into place, and I was in touch with Colonel Skeil's grandson, Alasdair, who was not able to get access to much family information. I also found out a good deal about Smith, though I was unhappy about the veracity of some of the details. At a late stage I was fortunate to be in touch with Professor Alan Sim, a volunteer at the Gordon Highlanders Museum in Aberdeen. We both helped each other and he was able to confirm what I had discovered elsewhere and provided more detail. That was a particularly satisfying conclusion to a research enquiry; happily there have been others.

My greatest difficulty has been over the illustrations, and my fear of using those still under copyright and requiring a licence. Those that might do so include the ones of Colonel Gordon (purchased from the Imperial War Museum), and the section reproduced from the group of Colonel Churchill and his officers which was made freely available for my use by Mr Tom Gordon (whose military rank I have not ascertained) at the Royal Scots Museum, Edinburgh Castle. It is taken from the *Magazine of the Royal Scots Fusiliers* for 1918. He also shrewdly identified Skeil from another group photograph in which he is not named, but could be recognised from wearing the regimental badges of the Royal Scots Fusiliers while serving in command of a unit of the Royal Scots, such is the privilege of officers on secondment, as was once my experience. The group photograph of Alastair Buchan with his platoon, and that of the Casualty Clearing Station are courtesy of The National Library of Scotland and were duly purchased. The photograph of Lieut. A. E. Buchan, M.A. is freely available by courtesy of the Hutchesons' Educational Trust Archives.

The website of The John Buchan Story in Peebles was an especially useful source, and acknowledgement is made for some of their photographs. Thanks are extended to its volunteers. The Chairman of Trustees, Ian Buckingham, was particularly helpful over providing photographs of the 2017 Rededication. Illustration 3 is by permission of Sauré, Lady Tweedsmuir through the courtesy of Ursula Buchan (see above), 7 by E. L. Hirst, and 39, photographed by Ian Buckingham is by favour of the Honourable Edward Buchan, as is that on the front cover. Cecilia Hope gave valuable assistance over one of the illustrations; and Dr Malcolm Golin, a member of The Heraldic Society, has made helpful suggestions and given permission to adapt drawings from his article on John Buchan's Heraldry in *The John Buchan Journal* (Illustrations 33-36). Peter Thackeray of Crask Books has been very supportive. Ursula Buchan and Mike Edwards, Vice-Chairman of the John Buchan Society have shown a kindly tolerance for the *e-mail*s to others, wrongly addressed to them. Hopefully they may find this resulting publication worth the trouble. The Covid-19 pandemic has caused difficulties in publishing which ended in a last minute problem with the cover. This was urgently resolved through the kindness of Seiko Angelo, copywriter in London, a friend of my younger son.

While some images are for sale under licence, others are in the public domain. I have made every effort to respect ownership, taking due care in producing this not for profit publication of limited academic interest and circulation. Any infringement of copyright was unintentional. I can only apologise, and will make any necessary amends. Having had the generous help of a number of people, they are in no way responsible for any errors that still remain here; these are entirely my own responsibility.

Kilmany   *D.W.*

Postscript: 19th November 2020

I am moved to add that this much delayed book also commemorates a long time reader of John Buchan,

Caroline Mayr-Harting
(14th June 1944 - 6th November 2020)

who was laid to rest in the Oxfordshire earth. She was the greatly beloved mother-in-law of my younger son, and it is only proper that her many kindnesses to us and her interest in my researches should be remembered in acknowledging support from others.

aeternam habeas requiem

3. The Buchan Family in 1909

The family was at the centre of the lives of the Buchans. Here Anna, William, Susan (covered) stand; the Reverend John, his wife Helen with Alice, and John sit; while Alastair and Walter are seated on the ground. (This is one of the last happy photographs with the parents, for when William next came on leave from India in 1912, Mr Buchan had died the previous year.)

The Importance of this Historical Study

"I have enormous admiration for those
such as yourself who narrate
previously unknown tales from the past
and present them to a new audience.
In the past we will discover the future."

(One of the archivists mentioned in the Introduction)

or

"If you don't know where you come from,
...you will never know where you are,
or where you are going."

(Buchan, J., *The Long Traverse*, 15)

and

Some will find Buchan too good for comfort
and, no doubt, will think likewise of Alastair.
Others will rightly recognise them as being
admirable religious, and moral role models for today,
and in the years to come.

(The Author)

CONTENTS

ILLUSTRATIONS

PREFACE

The writing of this book arose out of the continuing scholarly interest in John Buchan, well known as the author of *The Thirty-Nine Steps*, but deservedly remembered for much else. He died eighty years ago, but there have already appeared three full-length biographies (the most recent being published only in 2019). There have been a dozen or more other works about him and his writing. He and his siblings were very talented, and his father thought his brother William might "get to the top first." Alastair, and a little sister died prematurely young, but might also have had distinguished careers. They were a particularly loving and close-knit family of a timeless and strong Christianity. Some readers may be helped by first having an introduction to the individuals.

The Buchan Family

The Revd John, (1847-1911) Minister of the Free Church of Scotland, older brother of William, Town Clerk of Peebles.

Helen Jane, (1857-1937) his wife, a daughter of John Masterton of Broughton Green in the county of Peebles.

John, (1875-1940) gifted in many ways, noted author, and finally Governor-General of Canada, as Lord Tweedsmuir of Elsfield, Oxfordshire

Anna Masterton, (1877-1948) a noted writer as "O. Douglas".

William Henderson, (1880-1912) of the Indian Civil Service.

(James) Walter, (1883-1954) Town Clerk of Peebles and author.

Violet Katherine Stuart, (1888-1893).

Alastair Ebenezer, (1894-1917) of whom we treat.

* * * * *

The Royal Scots Fusiliers

1678 Raised as The Earl of Mar's Regiment of Foot
by Charles Erskine, 5th Earl of Mar

1686 became Buchan's Regiment of Foot after its Colonel

1689 known as O'Farrell's Fusiliers after its Colonel

1694 became the 21st Regiment of Foot

1707 at the Union became The North British Fusiliers

1713 became The Royal North British Fusiliers

1751 became the 21st Fusiliers (Royal North British)

1877-1959 The Royal Scots Fusiliers

Nickname: "The Duke of Marlborough's Own" after their formidable performance in Marlborough's campaigns during the War of Spanish Succession 1701-1713

Motto: *Nec Aspera Lacessit* (Hardships do not deter us); also used *Nemo Impune Lacessit* (No one provokes with impunity) from the Stuart Royal Arms of Scotland

March: "Highland Laddie", although latterly they were recruited from the Scottish Lowlands

Tartan: Hunting Erskine, presumably from the founder's family

Hackle: White plume

Bearskin: colloquially described as a busby, but only Fusilier Regiments & the Brigade of Guards wear these skins

Badge: The Royal Arms of the United Kingdom on a flaming grenade

The Regiment contributed nineteen battalions in the First World War, and lost between five and six thousand men. Caution is needed because there is always a danger of omissions in detailed assessments of such casualties and of exaggeration in generalisations.

*   *   *   *   *

"Fragment of an Ode
in Praise of the Royal Scots Fusiliers"

The poem printed overleaf was first published in 1917 by John Buchan, Alastair's eldest brother, in *Poems Scots and English*. Presumably, it was written before Alastair was killed in April. Nevertheless, it celebrates him in the regiment in which he served and died in action. The RSF had already fought with great distinction in battle at Mons, and his own 6th Battalion had done so at Loos, both times with great loss of life. There, and as the 6/7th RSF they fought on the Somme while Alastair was training troops in Scotland following repatriation after being wounded. He returned to the front line as that battle was ending. Buchan visited his brother more than once on the Western Front and talked with RSF veterans of Loos and of the Somme. Alastair died on the first day of the Battle of Arras.

"Fragment of an Ode
in Praise of the Royal Scots Fusiliers"

Ye'll a' hae heard tell o' the Fusilier Jocks,
   The famous auld Fusilier Jocks!
   They're as stieve as a stane,
   And as teuch as a bane,
  And as gleg as a pack of muircocks.
They're maistly as braid as they're lang,
And the Gairman's a pump off the fang
   When he faces the fire in their ee.
      They're no verra bonny,
      I question if ony
  Mair terrible sicht ye could see
Than a chairge o' the Fusilier Jocks.
      It gars Hindenburg swear
      "*Gott in Himmel*, nae mair
   O' thae sudden and scan'alous shocks!"
      And the cannon o' Krupp
      Ane and a' they shut up
Like a pentit bit jaick-in-the box,
At the rush o' the Fusilier Jocks.
The Kaiser he says to his son
    (The auld ane that looks like a fox)-
     "I went ower far
     When I stertit this war,
    Forgettin' the Fusilier Jocks.
 I could manage the French and Italians and Poles,
  The Russians and Tartars and yellow Mongols
The Serbs and the Belgians, the English and Greeks,
  And even the lads that gang wantin' the breeks ;
  But what o' thae Fusilier Jocks,
  That stopna for duntin' and knocks ?
    They'd rin wi' a yell
    Ower the plainstanes o' Hell ;
They're no men ava – they are rocks!
    They'd gang barefit
    Through the Bottomless Pit,
And they'll tak Berlin in their socks,-
Will thae terrible Fusilier Jocks!"
            John Buchan, 1917

Throughout the text

The Reverend John Buchan, the father, is referred to as

Mr Buchan

His wife as Helen

John Buchan (Lord Tweedsmuir) as

Buchan

His siblings by their Christian names

William

Anna

Walter

Violet

Alastair

Buchan's wife is referred to as Susan or
occasionally later as Lady Tweedsmuir

CHAPTER ONE

INTRODUCTION

Alastair was the youngest in the family. They were the five surviving children of the Reverend John Buchan and his wife Helen. He was the shortest lived, never celebrating his twenty-third birthday. All four brothers went on from Hutchesons' Grammar School to the University of Glasgow. John and William continued with their education at Brasenose College, in Oxford, and Walter was destined for the Scottish Bar.

They all showed early promise of distinguished careers. Their sister, Anna, writing as "O. Douglas" became a very successful author between the world wars. Because of the brevity of his life Alastair can

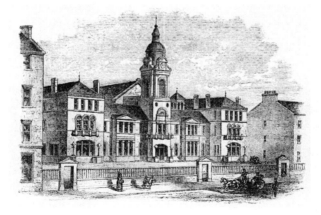

4. Hutchesons'

easily be dismissed as the least able of them all, lacking ambition and apparently entering on a career in accountancy, which does not seem to predict much eminence to come. That may not be a fair judgement. Any promise of making his mark later was curtailed by his gallant early death and his story deserves to be more fully told.

It is unlikely that so brief a life would be much chronicled, but there are a number of sources. A small box of paper memorabilia, no doubt gathered in his home, is archived.[1] His sister, Anna, was responsible for three published accounts. She was fourteen years older and had a good deal to do with his mothering. Immediately after his death she wrote a privately printed memorial book, *Alastair Buchan 1894-1917*. Though one would like to know even more, there are some references to him in her reminiscences, *Unforgettable, Unforgotten*, but many of them repeat what she had said earlier. She also represented him in some of her fiction.[2] A little more may be gleaned from other books by her brother John and widow, Susan, and her nephew William and his daughter Ursula, while family members might have other material not deposited in the public domain. (See also Endnote on page 6). Ursula was recently surprised by such in writing about her great uncle William, I.C.S.

---

[1] National Library of Scotland, (NLS) Acc.11627/37.
[2] Buchan, A., *Unforgettable*, 155; Thomas, "France, 1992", 14.

Walter was his closest brother, but still eleven years senior, while there was a nineteen-year gap between John and this youngest of the brothers. Anna said that "it is not blood the Buchans have in their veins, it is ink."[3] That was true of her, their father, and three of her brothers who were all published writers. Even their Uncle Willie contributed to the *Journal of the Society of Antiquaries of Scotland.* Alastair might have joined them in such activity for he loved books and poetry, but he never had much chance apart from writing for his University magazine.[4]

There is one reservation about using the sources on Alastair's life. Most of the anecdotes about him come from his eldest brother John (hereinafter referred to as Buchan) and his sister, Anna. They were deeply emotionally involved in their grieving for him, and knew that beneath the carefree humour there was a vulnerability in him which he had joked about, as we shall see. They were greatly moved therefore by the accounts of others who wrote of his gallant behaviour on the day of his death in encouraging his men before the attack and thereafter. When recording it, Anna suddenly burst out, "Our *little* boy." He had been their beloved kid brother, replacing an adored sister who had died tragically young. For Buchan, this had been

---

[3] Quoted in Cowan, J., *Canada's Governors-General*, 163.
[4] Buchan, A., *Alastair Buchan*, 14; Buchan's four children showed the same propensity, as do some of their descendants. Apart from books, Walter wrote reviews for *The Spectator*.

largely at a distance as he had left home when Alastair was a year old. For Anna it was with the intimacy of being virtually a surrogate mother who nevertheless did not supplant Helen in his maternal affection. [5]

However, there are several factors which mitigate against any over emotional and personal bias in these writings. Though better on feelings than facts,

5. Alastair with Anna

Anna frequently quotes directly from letters, the originals of which often survive. Some of her anecdotes are repeated later in life or corroborated by Buchan or other family members. Wide-ranging tributes from civilians as well as soldiers all show Alastair to have been an exceptionally attractive person. When the remaining siblings did occasionally romanticise a little about what he had done, that is understandable as symptoms of an underlying reality for they had their vulnerabilities, too.

---

[5] Buchan, A., *Alastair Buchan*, 41.

Having now lost their beloved father, and three of their siblings, Buchan had become painfully ill, and there was concern about their mother's erratic health. Life was precarious for other reasons as well. They were in the middle of an unprecedentedly terrible war. Everything seemed under threat, Buchan had already lost close friends and would lose more, Anna mourned the brother she had loved to mother, and too many young neighbours. If there is a tendency for them to glamorise his sacrifice, Buchan especially in his poem, Anna perhaps in her remembrances, we just have to factor this in. Moreover, it does not have to affect the veracity of what now follows.

This account endeavours to represent the salient points in several sources, including Anna's memorial book which is much quoted here, not being widely known, together with added comment and illustrative background information. Even taking into account the eulogistic notices following his tragically early death, Alastair does seem to have been a particularly attractive young man, and faithful to what were then regarded as very high standards of behaviour in his personal life and especially mindful of the welfare of others. Anna summed it up as "the rounded, perfect, complete life that was his. Twenty-two years of straightness and gentleness and mirth." Today, it may seem rather priggish to many, but then it would have been widely applauded as admirable and much to be emulated, "and then came the end. And such an end!"

We shall find that the admiration of his peers is particularly significant in assessing his cheerful and gallant character. This must have been especially apparent to them in the constant daily round of danger, often in very miserable conditions, as much as amid the little real battle experience that he was to see. "So....he passed, young-eyed and joyous, through the wicket gate at the end of the Way."[6]

Endnote: About Sources & Why "O. Douglas?"

About Sources: these for Alastair's life are mention on page 2. I know too little about others. The website of The John Buchan Story in Peebles has copies of some photographs and letters concerning Alastair which I have used. During the last year in which I have been writing this, it has been virtually impossible for me to travel. People of my generation find no substitute for being able to visit sources in person. Failing to do this in Peebles makes me fear that there may be further information deposited there that I have not seen. Time presses, prospects of travel do not improve, so I leave it to others to fill in my deficiencies. (See also, 198 below for *Farewell to Priorsford*.)

Why "O. Douglas?": for lack of space, the note which was appropriate here can be found on page 196ff. below.

---

[6] Buchan, A., *Alastair Buchan*, 41.

CHAPTER TWO

SURPRISES IN HIS PRE-WAR DAYS

There are at least four particular surprises about Alastair by the time he was twenty. But first something must be said about the man and the family circumstances into which he was born on the twelfth of June 1894 at Florence Villa, 24 Queen Mary Avenue, the family home in Glasgow. There was no manse for the Minister of John Knox Free Church of Scotland, which was two miles away in the Gorbals, and so Mr Buchan, the father, had to buy his own

6. Florence Villa

house. It was detached and in the pleasant residential district of Cathcart. Besides the three older brothers, and Anna, there had been a younger sister, the adored baby of the family [November 1888 - June 1893]. They were bereaved when she was four, so that "nothing was ever quite the same after Violet's death, certainly not to her parents."[7] Alastair was conceived in the immediate aftermath of this tragically early loss. With his siblings all more than ten years older, he very naturally filled the gap as the beloved baby of them all, though John Buchan left for Oxford when he was still a toddler, and was little at home thereafter. The two must have known each other best when Alastair was a young adult and a much loved fledgling uncle to Buchan's older children, Alice and John.

The first surprise has already been touched on. While Buchan later regarded Alastair almost as his eldest child, to Anna he was almost a son: "from the first he belonged specially to me" because their mother was "busy with a multitude of things." Given his isolation in age, he grew up to be a rather self-contained child, readily entertaining himself, but very engaging. Here the principal reporter must be Anna, who was continuously present during the first decade of his life. She says that "he was a plain baby, and grew into a very plain little boy, with a rather Mongolian cast of countenance...."[8]

Now we must discuss his name. Mr Buchan registered the birth with Grozier, the Cathcart Registrar on the fourth of July. The surviving

---

[7] Buchan, A., *Unforgettable*, 17.
[8] Ibid., 67.

document seems inexplicable for it was issued in the Christian names of "Allister [sic] Ebenezer Masterton." Perhaps this was due to Mr Buchan's well known vagueness over detail. The Registrar must have been very familiar with Alastair and its variants Alistair and Alasdair, the last being a corruption of the Norman-French which became Alexander in English. Mr Buchan had a rather estranged brother called Alexander. As with Walter, the third son, it did not have to have been a family name, but the mother had a much loved brother called Ebenezer, only six years older than John and the two were very close friends. It was a natural choice; so was Masterton because it was Helen Buchan's surname, just as William's second name was Henderson after his paternal grandmother. In spite of this very close family association, it was dropped from the full name by which he was later known and does not seem to have been used again.

Perhaps Mr Buchan added it as a tribute to his wife and in celebration of her bearing new life after the death of Violet. They already had a daughter Anna Masterton Buchan, and on reflection it may have been thought unnecessary to give a family name to Alastair as well. The baptismal records for Mr Buchan's church are not in the public domain, and may not have survived.[9] Certainly he was entered at Hutchesons' in the name of "Alastair Ebenezer Buchan" and in

---

[9] Information received after enquiries at the National Archives of Scotland (January 2019).

records thereafter. Presumably he could have later used his full name as registered, had he so wished. There are other curious things about his name. Christened Alastair:

> He was seldom called by that name. The first time John saw him [he was absent at his birth] he said, "Hullo! Peter." And Peter he was for the first few years. When he began to develop a personality of his own he was re-named "the Mhor" – the Gaelic for "the great one." Thus was greatness thrust upon him.[10]

Buchan's reaction is interesting in that he used the name later for some of his fictional heroes: Richard Hannay's son, Peter John, and Pineaar and Pentecost were also Peter. He liked such forms of remembrance in his stories.[11] Seeming delicate as an infant, he would become "a big, broad-shouldered, fresh-coloured boy." His upbringing was surrounded by loving adults but lacking close peers. He had a fertile imagination which provided his own entertainment.[12] Anna's revelations are rich in anecdotal stories and sayings from his childhood. At the age of seven, he was young to have experienced wartime South Africa

---

[10] Buchan, A., *Unforgettable*, 67; cf. *Alastair Buchan*, 7.

[11] Especially in *The Island of Sheep* (1935). Pineaar in earlier books, Pentecost in *The Blanket of the Dark* (1931). Peter is the kid brother in *The Magic Walking Stick* (1932).

[12] Buchan, A., *Alastair Buchan*, 7-9.

with his parents (1901-1902), bringing back a mongoose called "Rikki", and he was the most widely travelled child in the family. Anna wrote in reminiscence that it was

absurd that that child should have so many treats – trips to Switzerland and France, motor tours, fortnights in London hotels – things we never dreamed of having – but it was just as if we were allowed to give him every single pleasure we could think of that we might be glad afterwards.

There is evidence from postcards sent to Walter, of a holiday in the Lake District. In 1905, Alastair was only eleven, yet with two other boys he reports walking twenty miles on a Tuesday, including a noted climb. After doing less the next day, they concluded the holiday covering thirty miles, the last fifteen in less than four hours. He acknowledges that Walter would have empathised with such exploits, as would his other siblings.[13]

The next surprise is that on the 9th September 1907 Alastair was entered at Hutchesons' not from a Glasgow school, but from Peebles High School some fifty miles distant. Whenever the decision was made to send him away from his parental home to school in Peebles it was probably when Buchan's Uncle Willie died in February 1906. Helen being fully engaged with

---

[13] Buchan, A., *Alastair Buchan*, 17; NLS, Acc. 11627/76a; postcards 18th, 25th August & 1st September 1905.

other duties, Anna had been at home in Glasgow with her parents mothering Alastair.

She moved into Bank House with Walter and it was natural enough for her young brother to move with her until he returned home to go to the same day school as his brothers. Ursula Buchan gives a delightful account of how Alastair behaved when Buchan's fiancée, Susan Grosvenor, first met the Peebles family in late May 1907. Wearing his kilt and a ribboned cap, his first words were a welcoming, "Very glad to see you", and she had reason to be grateful to him thereafter.

He was unaffectedly delighted to make her acquaintance [unlike his mother] and was

7. Bank House, Peebles

prepared to bake her cakes as tokens of his esteem.... Even disregarding the exaggerations prompted by family affection, he was plainly a delightful boy: funny, cheerful, idiosyncratic, a great dreamer, and much attached to his family. He was a voracious reader of poetry and prose.[14]

Earlier he had been equivocal about his family. Though his father was a minister and he was encouraged to follow him, he declined saying that it was "not a white man's job." He disliked the Sabbath, and angels, wanting "to be a jockey." Conscious of acting before the gallery of Buchan's visiting Oxford undergraduate friends he once said,

I was playing quietly in Heaven one day when God came and said to me, "Mohr, you're going to live with the Buchans." I said, *"The Buchans, Good Lord!"...* [mimicking their] Oxford drawl.[15]

The other details on Alastair's record of Admission to Hutchesons' are as would be expected, except that his home address is not registered as being at Florence Villa, 24 Queen Mary Avenue. This is frequently assumed to have been their family home throughout their time in Glasgow. It was not.

About 1903, they moved to another house

---

[14] Buchan, U., *Beyond*, 131 & 133.
[15] Buchan, A, *Alastair Buchan*, 10-11. "Mhor" is misspelt throughout. Nightmare of family on a ship bound for Hell, ibid.

called Thornwood at 36 Maxwell Drive, Pollok-
shields, possibly a little nearer to their Church.[16] It was
no more than a decade old, and more convenient. John
had left home years before, William was off to India,
Walter to study for the Bar, leaving the parents with
Anna and Alastair. They could not know that for over
a year in 1906-07, after the death of Mr Buchan's

*8. Houses opposite 36 Maxwell Drive
(since demolished)*

---

[16] There are a number of postcards sent to various members of
the family at Maxwell Drive between April 1905 and August
1906 (NLS Acc. 11627/47) as well as this use of it a year later.
Clarification comes from the *Post Office Glasgow Directory for
Glasgow*. The edition for 1903-1904 (preface dated May 1903)
shows the minister of John Knox Church still at Queen Mary
Avenue (110), (and a letter in August, 139, note 176), but that
the house was already in other hands with four men listed in the
street directory (905), where 36 Maxwell Drive was left blank
(858). This indicates that the move was in progress around the
time of publication and probably just too late for inclusion.

brother Willie, their parents would be on their own when Anna went off to Peebles to keep house for Walter, taking Alastair along with her until he moved back and started at Hutchesons'. He left that school three years later in June 1910 at the age of sixteen. At the time, this was not at all unusual among his contemporaries, when they had achieved the necessary certificate to move on. [17] It was also natural enough since his parents had just retired to Peebles, though it was another year before he entered the University of Glasgow.

9. Woodlands,
Peebles

Probably he spent time at the house that his brothers had bought for their parents. It was called "Woodlands." In the spring of 1910 his father became an invalid and his mother was seriously ill that

[17] Personal communication from the Archivist (Julie Devenney), 7th May 2019.

autumn, around the time when he was leaving school. Their new home was very close to Bank House.[18]

Then we come to the question of Alastair's lack of purpose in life. Buchan, perhaps predictably, somewhat romanticises in his memorial poem:

> *You made no careful plans for life,*
> *Happy with dreams and books and friends,*
> *Incurious of our earthly strife,*
> *As dedicate to nobler ends.*[19]

Though understandable, this may lead to some misinterpretation. His older brothers seemed to know early in life the general direction they wanted it to take. Buchan had settled on the law by the time he left Oxford, but soon deviated into other directions. William appears to have been single-minded about the Indian Civil Service, just as Walter was about the law, though we may not know enough about their early career "growing pains." Alastair had rejected the idea that he should be a minister,[20] or a jockey and was early denied a real ambition of his own.

In 1922, one of the men who had been prominent in the Glasgow congregation was in correspondence with Anna about her memorial volume. He recalled how he had once asked Mr

---

[18] Buchan, U., *Beyond*, 144.
[19] Buchan, A., *Unforgettable*, 150; for the quotation see below, 99.
[20] Buchan, A., *Alastair Buchan*, 10.

Buchan what Alastair would do in life. His father answered with utter clarity, "He wants to be a soldier."

10. "To be a soldier"

Later on, and after his father's death, Anna recalled oddly, that

> it was difficult to decide on a profession for our little brother.... [as though it was something to be left to John and the others.] The Army and Navy were vetoed by mother as being "too dangerous"; it must not be India, for we couldn't part from our baby.[21]

In the end, despite supposedly taking "very little interest in his own future,"[22] Alastair was not aimless. It had been strongly suggested that he too should

---

[21] Buchan, A., *Alastair Buchan*, 15.
[22] Ibid., 15; Buchan, A., *Unforgettable*, 138.

follow the established male Buchan course and study law. In three generations, this had been their first choice of career, for only Uncle Tom, and brother William had deviated from it. While taking his final university examinations, he wrote to his mother saying firmly that he had settled on accountancy, He did not believe in "the Mathematical mind". All that was required was an aptitude for figures and he had been "fairly good at school at Maths." Three years before he had passed the Prelims, and did not anticipate problems with taking the finals. On completing his third year at Glasgow, he only spent a short time in Mr Maxtone Graham's office in Edinburgh, starting in June 1914.[23] He may have been mistaken in this ambition, but in the event it did not signify. Within the briefest space of time world events enabled him to achieve his first wish and revel in its fulfilment.

Endnote on Accountancy.

Alastair's decision on accountancy is stated in his letter to his mother from 1 Garden Street, W, n.d., evidently in 1914 just after taking exams, NLS Acc.11627/37. James Maxtone Graham (of the Lairds of Cultoquhey, Perthshire for six hundred years) founded the firm of Maxtone Graham & Sime, Charlotte Square, Edinburgh, "one of the most respected firms of accountants in Scotland." Being articled to such a prestigious firm was probably engineered by Alastair's older brothers; Buchan, A., *Alastair Buchan*, 16; *Unforgettable*, 145.

---

[23] Buchan, A., *Alastair Buchan*, 16.

There remains a slight uncertainty about whether entering Maxtone Graham's office really meant that he would pursue a career in that profession. Not very encouragingly, Anna commented on his personal attempt at book-keeping: "Alastair Buchan in account with self", was "much ornamented with funny faces (he was quite a fair caricaturist) and not very accurate, sums are often noted as 'lost.' It stops suddenly with the scrawl, 'The War here intervened.'" *Alastair Buchan*, 16. When David Maxwell Fyfe (afterwards the Earl of Kilmuir) remembered his youthful impression of Buchan at tea parties, he said that he himself had prepared for the Bar by brief experience in offices of accountants and solicitors, Kilmuir, *Memoirs*, 23-24. Fyfe wrote this having retired as Lord Chancellor, so it was likely for a fledging lawyer to do that. Perhaps Buchan and Walter retained a residual hope that Alastair would move on to the law once he had briefly experienced accountancy.

CHAPTER THREE

THE UNIVERSITY OF GLASGOW

11. University of Glasgow main entrance

Here is Anna's account of Alastair's time as a Glasgow student:

About his three years at college there is not much to say. He joined the Fabian Society to the amusement of his brothers, he wrote articles for the University Magazine, he passed his examinations with credit, and he made many friends.

A contemporary wrote that "there was no one in his year at College more generally beloved than Alastair." While there "I never met anyone more honourable, more careless of spending himself for others more fearless of fighting any ugly injustice than he was." [24]

There are some misunderstandings within the family about Alastair during the last three months of 1914 that have been chronicled. These concern his withdrawal from college, and have been fuelled by things that Buchan or his sister recorded.

Though Buchan implies that his brother volunteered at the outbreak of war (4th August), it was not before 19th October 1914 that Alastair was sent a postcard calling him for his medical back in Glasgow.[25] Then as a member of the University Officers' Training Corps he would have been fast-tracked for a commission, but they thought that he was not at first keen to apply for one because he enjoyed too much the company of his fellow "squaddies".[26]

---

[24] Buchan, A., *Alastair Buchan*, 14. One of his great friends was "a very brilliant scholar" 2/Lieut. Peter Purdie, M.C. who was kllled four months after Alastair: Anna to Susie, Broughton Green, 22nd August 1917, JB Story Archive.

[25] Buchan, J., *Memory-Hold-the-Door*, 255; NLS Acc. 11627/37.

[26] Buchan, A., *Alastair Buchan*, 18.

Though not explicitly stated, it is likely that he was a member of the Officers' Training Corps. Some of Anna's comments seem to assume that he was and, having left home, that would be consistent with his own compensating for a frustrated military ambition. It would also be compatible with his being commissioned within no more than four months.

There were not a few public school men who felt they could serve more usefully in the ranks. The most notable of these was Buchan's friend, the Earl of Crawford and Balcarres (Eton), who declined to be Viceroy of India and then enlisted as a private in the Medical Corps. Among many others was H. H. "Saki" Munro (Bedford), the writer, who died as a Sergeant in the Royal Fusiliers. Buchan has an interesting take on this in *Mr Standfast*, creating Lancelot Wake. This gentleman pacifist (cousin of Mary Lamington) and British secret agent enlists in the ranks, serving in various non-combatant capacities until he volunteers directly under Hannay. Still a pacifist, he dies heroically ensuring the success of the combatants. We can be sure that Alastair was not among those intent on delaying or avoiding being commissioned.

There was also the conviction that he had already graduated as a Master of Arts before he joined up. We have seen that Anna remembered when War was declared that Alastair was still involved with the University, but "he took his degree in October, and went off at once to train with the O.T.C. somewhere in England."[27] The postcard, soon quoted, also seems to imply that he was a member of the Corps at the University. Once in camp at Bramshott it may be that Alastair had written casually to the family that being so attached to his fellows in the ranks he was not keen to become an officer but, still, once commissioned "everyone he came into contact with was 'a capital fellow.'" He "was one of those happy souls whose path through life is lined with friends, and whose kind eyes met only affectionate looks." [28]

The best way to resolve most of the confusion is to set out a reconstruction of the events of his last few days before he left Scotland to go to war.

Monday 19th October: A postcard was sent to him in Peebles from the Glasgow University Contingent of the Cameron Highlanders telling him to present himself at the Physiology Department for a medical examination on the Wednesday or Thursday.[29]

Tuesday 20th October: the postcard was received in Peebles; Alastair returned to Glasgow.

Wednesday 21st October: He passed the medical; he signed the "Attestation for a three year Short Service commission" as a "Student" and

---

[27] Buchan, A., *Unforgettable*, 145-146.
[28] Buchan, A., *Alastair Buchan*, 18.
[29] Monday & Friday from the postcard to be found in NLS Acc.11627/37; Wednesday & Thursday from documents at Kew.

as Private No.14706 in the Cameron Highlanders.

Thursday 22nd October: Back in Peebles Alastair got his mother to sign a form for the "Nomination of Candidate for appointment to a Temporary Commission" as a "Student", (he, being under twenty-one). Alastair also signed. Rather surprisingly it says he could not ride a horse.[30] He returned to Glasgow.

Friday 23rd October: He left Glasgow by train for Aldershot.

These details confirm that Alastair was called for a medical by the Glasgow O.T.C.; that he was still a student when he left home and that, whatever his siblings thought his mother knew that he had not graduated. He had just enlisted as a soldier (with his army number) and had already made his application to be considered for a commission.

It remains to question why some of the family were convinced that Alastair did take his degree, and indeed some captions to his photograph credit him with being an "M.A." This seems to emanate from information supplied by some of them to Hutchesons' and passed on to the University for their Roll of honour, where it was used without checking.

---

[30] Copies of these two documents are in his Officer's Records at Kew. Re: "could not ride" – unlikely after so many visits to Broughton, & Anna in *Unforgettable*, 146 – "rode to dinner." Perhaps he was determined to avoid a cavalry posting.

Graduating in October would explain waiting until late in that month before enlisting in the army. However, on checking with the University Archivist, it appears that his file is kept as "an abandoned one" which indicates that his studies were never completed. On the Roll of Honour he is described as "Student". No record could be found that he had ever graduated, despite an exhaustive check.[31] The family were very used to having graduates among them, and are unlikely to have been mistaken, yet the University archives, as well as the *Calendar*, contain no record of a degree ever having been conferred upon him.[32]

The most likely explanation for this odd discrepancy seems to be this. He had expected to graduate without Honours at Glasgow hoping to go on to Oxford like two of his brothers, but he did not win a scholarship.[33] Perhaps on the rebound from that late news he decided to enrol for a fourth year at Glasgow,

---

[31] Personal communication from Laura Burchell, Archive Assistant, 9th May 2019, abandoned file ref. R6/10. The *University of Glasgow Calendar 1915-16* lists "Degrees conferred in the various Faculties… from 21st April 1914 to 20th April 1915" do not include Alastair.

[32] Until May 2019, the University online "Roll of Honour" included a photograph, "source unknown", with the caption "Lieut. A. E. Buchan, M.A." It seems to have been taken from the *Hutchesons' Magazine*, and probably supplied by the family, who will also have suggested the caption.

[33] Personal communication from Ursula Buchan, December 2019.

and try again for Oxford. The matter is of no great
significance except that if he entered an accountant's
office before completing his studies at Oxford or
Glasgow, it may have been to gain experience rather
than to begin training for a career.

Though it seems odd that some of his family
were misled, these events happened just after War had
broken out and Alastair was bustling to go off to fight.
Though his mother was aware that he had not

Lieut. Alastair E. Buchan, M.A.

12. The wrong "M.A." caption

graduated, perhaps the siblings did not realise the
change of plan. It remains a curiosity, especially since
Anna first says that "in the Summer of 1914, he took

his degree"[34] (i.e. before commencing with Maxtone Graham). It is also possible that his mother did share that misconception, but thought that when she signed him off as a student for his commission he had changed his mind after graduating and had enrolled for Honours. In that case he was once more a student. She may also have been too distressed at his joining up to notice what she was signing in the document.

Endnote on Appreciations of Alastair (cf. 21 & Ch. 10)

The Reverend John Buchan would have been pleased to hear about the kindness and concern for others shown by his sons, having spent himself in that way. Buchan was noted for his many kindnesses, just as Alastair was said to be "careless of spending himself for others" (21). This is echoed by what was said of William in India: "his visits were looked forward to by the people he tried to help" and "There was an atmosphere about him more clean, more straight, more brave than I have met with elsewhere.... A type dear to the imagination but so seldom met with in the flesh.... he was the one I would have gone to in any deep trouble or distress of mind or body." He did his "work from higher motives than most of us." This testimony to William by a colleague in India (Anna's *Unforgettable, Unforgotten*, 137) could be applied elsewhere among this family of Buchans.

---

[34] Buchan, A., *Alastair Buchan*, 15 – at variance with her account on 22-23, note 27: "He took his degree in October."

CHAPTER FOUR

HIS LITERARY INTERESTS

Anna say he "wasn't in the least a precocious child.[35] That may be so, yet he had some of the scholarly interests of his brothers, since from an early age he showed an advanced appreciation of literature. Like the rest of the family, Alastair evidently found great pleasure in reading. In an age devoid of present advances in media distractions this was no doubt naturally fuelled by his environment, and by spending a lot of time in his own company, but nevertheless its fruits seem remarkable in one so young.

The family rejoiced in Alastair's "original sayings, in his curious dreaming ways, in his passion for poetry." At the age of five he had *The Midsummer Night's Dream* and *Twelfth Night* "almost by heart", and he had *Morte D'Arthur* read to him at bedtime. His habit of walking up and down while telling himself stories aloud disconcerted some visitors who thought him "not quite right". (This notable habit continued throughout his adulthood, when he would similarly read poetry or a passage from a favourite book.) Buchan recalled that when Alastair

---

[35] Buchan, A., *Alastair Buchan*, 8.

was a child he was a devotee of *Cyrano de Bergerac*, [which he never tired of] and his favourite scene was that "under the walls of Arras." [Standing on the back of the sofa] I remember how he would declaim, "Who are these men that rush on death?" and [then with a wave of his sword he would leap off] thunder[ing] forth the answer, "Cadets of Gascony are we." He did not dream that it would be his fate to fall on an April morning under the walls of Arras.

In his memorial poem Buchan remembered him as being "Happy with dreams and books and friends."[36]

When it came to the War, Alastair, newly commissioned, was paid seven shillings and six pence a day: "I think I can live quite well on it. I don't spend much money and have never spent more than two shillings a day... except in buying books, etc."[37] He and his friend Stevenson (see below, 34) were greatly entertained by O. Henry's stories, and what we know about his reading as a subaltern in France shows a considerable width of intellectual interest. Susan sent

---

[36] Buchan's indented account, *Memory-Hold-the-Door*, 255-256, is interspersed with Anna's, first published in *Alastair Buchan*, 8-10. She added, "On the evening of Easter Sunday 1917 [as he] waited with his men at Arras to attack at dawn.... Did he remember, I wonder?"

[37] Letter to mother, n.d. from Pembroke College. NLS Acc.11627/37.

him Chesterton's *Poems*, which he had long time loved, and he could engage in argument with his fellow men about Stonewall Jackson.[38]

The last books he was reading were Gilbert Murray's *Hippolytus, The Bacchae* by Euripides, and Belloc's *Path to Rome.*[39] If the last were an attempt to convert the reader to that faith it would have alarmed some of his family. In fact it is a delightful account of a pilgrimage "to see all Europe which the Christian faith has saved." His determination to remain true to his father's Christian faith and teaching is shown by his reaction to receiving from the family a "little prayer book". In thanking them he wrote, "One's body gets so filthy here that the only thing to do is to keep one's mind and soul as clean as possible."[40]

After his death, and among his private papers in his desk at home, there was found a poem. Previously unknown to his family, it bears the date September 1912 and was composed as he started on his second year as an undergraduate. Written perhaps after his ambition to become a soldier had been vetoed

---

[38] Buchan, A., *Alastair Buchan*, 19, 29, 9, & 26-27.

[39] In her letter Anna to Buchan, Peebles 7th May 1917, JB Story Archive, she says that "the Gilbert Murray books have come back" with Alastair's kit, and offers them to Susie, Buchan's wife, because "he had evidently treasured them." It sounds as though the Murrays, who had mentored Buchan, had been in touch with him.

[40] Buchan, A., *Alastair Buchan*, 29, 31, & 26.

by his mother, it uses a military and Christian metaphor. Nevertheless, it may even more appropriately be seen to have had a general application. It also has a timeless quality which makes it relevant to a Christian in any age.

The poem was first printed in Anna's memorial volume as

The Crusader's Prayer

O Lord, I pray for strength to fight
Thy battles in this world below:
Teach me to choose not wrong but right;
May he who hates Thee be my foe.[41]

Teach me, I pray, the ways of truth,
Of gentleness, and charity,
That I may live as He who died,
Slain by mankind upon the tree.

And may I learn, O God, to love
This world which Thou hast given me;
And may I use my life as seems
Most befitting, Lord, to Thee.

Help me to live a soldier's life,
Always with Thee to lean upon:

---

[41] But he did not hate "foes", see 122, note 165.

Faithful and hopeful to obey
The Captain of my Salvation. [42]

And when at length Death is at hand,
May I the last foe meet with pride,
And boldly and with eye undimmed
Out on my last adventure ride.

There was another very apt posthumous remembrance of him when his sister founded the Alastair Buchan Prize for Poetry at the University of Glasgow in 1919 (see pages 115-116). Then in 2017, the Great War Project there hosted an evening of music and poetry in his honour (page 126 & 127).

---

[42] Buchan, A., *Alastair Buchan*, 42-43. It was found at home in his desk after he had died. As early as 1896 Buchan had published a story called "a Captain of Salvation". It was not republished until 1996 and Alastair may not have known of it. It is irrelevant here since the phrase was common enough among Christians to refer to Jesus , and it fitted with Alastair's military imagery here. He will have got the symbolism of the Christian as a soldier from the New Testament (KJV), cf. *Ephesians* 6: 10-20: 2 *Timothy* 2, 3-5.

CHAPTER FIVE

ALASTAIR AND THE FIRST WORLD WAR:
1914-1915

Anna wrote that

> looking back we could see that Alastair had been
> born for the Great War.... He never seemed to be
> much interested in his own future, but to live in
> the present, always contented and gay.

Buchan agreed.[43] Their youngest brother joined with
the final draft from the University, with many men of
his year, leaving Glasgow for Aldershot on Friday,
23rd October. [44]

From there he was sent for basic training to the
camp outside of Bramshott, said to be the most
haunted village in Hampshire, and near Liphook. [45]
Conditions were primitive, with poor food, leaking
huts, and awful mud, though he made no complaint,
even at his uniform. Initially it was an 1880 red tunic
far too big, and equally unsuitable blue trousers. There

---

[43] Buchan, A., *Unforgettable*, 145. In these confused times, it
must be added that Anna was not indicating sexuality; Buchan,
J., *Memory-Hold-the-Door*, 255.
[44] NLS Acc 11627/37; Buchan, A., *Unforgettable*, 142.
[45] Buchan, J., *Memory-Hold-the-Door*, 255; Postcard in NLS
Acc. 11627/37; Buchan, A., *Unforgettable*, 146.

is an amusing letter to his mother about this time thanking her for the food parcels with which he was inundated. He sends a list of what would be best - but not too often![46]

13. "Steve"

Anna says that Alastair's great army friend was someone who he called "Steve", and that "they were together all through their training."[47] This needs some qualification. Thomas Kerr Stevenson came from Beith in Ayrshire, a son of the headmaster of Greenhills School, and was educated at Spier's School. It had recently been founded by a local benefactor as a secondary school to serve the parishes

---

[46] Alastair to mother, 8th Platoon, B Company, 6 Cameronians, Bramshott Camp, n.d., JB Story Archive.
[47] Buchan, A., *Alastair Buchan*, 19.

in the area, and it had extensive grounds which included gardens and sports fields. In less than a hundred years the rather fine stone building would be woefully swept away when replaced by a Comprehensive.

"Steve" matriculated at St Andrews on a Russell Bursary in 1912, joined the Officers' Training Corps, and represented the University at rugby and cricket. Anna says that "he was a brilliant scholar", but his studies as an Honours Arts student were interrupted at Martinmas 1914. He was commissioned from the Officers' Training Corps on 24th November 1914 when Alastair was only beginning his basic training.[48] They could not have known each other until they were both subalterns at Sutton Veny some months later.

As early as December 1915, before his brother was commissioned, Buchan was scheming to get him posted to a battalion of The Somerset Light Infantry commanded by the great friend of the family, Colonel Cecil Rawling. He even successfully enlisted the aid of his Oxford friend, Harold Baker (now an M.P.), in this attempt at manipulation but it still failed, and so Alastair was posted to a Scottish regiment.[49]

---

[48] *London Gazette*, 24th November 1914, No.28984, p.9695. The photograph is from Lang, *Roll of Honour*.
[49] Buchan to Baker, 10th January 1915: National Archives, Kew WO 339/26528. There are several letters in the JB Story Archive about this & Alastair's doubts.

In those early stages of the War those selected who had been in the O.T.C. were assumed to have the necessary leadership skills. If successful in initial training, they were commissioned and then given a month's military training in the arts of war. These courses were held in a number of places and individuals had no choice where they were sent. Alastair seems to have had this essential background for he received a letter at Bramshott telling him of his commission as a temporary Second Lieutenant with effect from the 22nd February 1915. Although initially in the Cameron Highlanders, he was assigned to the 8th Battalion, Royal Scots Fusiliers and not posted straight there but to "the class at Cambridge" beginning on the 3rd March. A letter from Alastair to his mother survives which, though undated, is early in

14. Old Court, Pembroke College
Cambridge

1915 from the context and is simply headed "Pembroke College".[50] This needs to be explained.

On the outbreak of War, the Vice-Chancellor at Cambridge, Montague Rhodes James, put the Colleges at the service of the Government. Oxford was slower to react. As early as December 1914 "the Cambridge University School of Instruction" was being held at Pembroke College. Alastair probably attended the third of these courses. It was soon evident that longer was needed. In 1916 the class length was increased to four months. That was equivalent to two University terms and candidates then became more like quasi-undergraduates, even engaging in bumping races on the river. For many, this time was an unbelievable break from the War. One of the candidates, Basil Willey, who became a don at Pembroke, described his first ever experience: "being in Cambridge, and yet not of it, I could drink in its beauty with the uncomplicated zest of a holiday-maker."

Even on a short course, Alastair would have enjoyed something of this experience. He will have dined in Hall and been made free of the Union. In town he will have enjoyed the bookshops and browsed the stalls in the Market Place with their striped awnings and magically lit by flares. He will have been impressed by Wren's Chapel at Pembroke, and by

---

[50] Commission: letter from Colonel E. W. M. Norie, John Buchan Story Archive; NLS Acc.11627/37 for letter to mother.

King's. The Backs, little built up on the far side in those days, and Coe Fen will have given a sense of the countryside. The poet Siegfried Sassoon had a similar experience later in the year.

The hundred or so men on a course shared two or three in a room; training was intensive, with days long and arduous. Though not unenjoyable for the young and fit; "for the literally minded they were undoubtedly dull", though there was also some free time. No records survive of these early days apart from personal memories. The later longer courses are well documented. Alastair will have enjoyed even briefly emulating his two older brothers at Oxbridge, and not been disappointed at ploughing his own furrow at "the other place."[51] It gave him a new experience. Thereafter he got on well with all ranks after he joined his battalion who were training at Sutton Veny, near Warminster. [52] Keen to be seen to be self-sufficient, he wrote home soon afterwards to say that his pistol

---

[51] Willey's quote and much detail in this paragraph come from two articles in the *Pembroke College Cambridge Annual Gazette*, September 2018: "'Tommy' and 'Sassons' at Pembroke: the legacy of 'Paradise'" by Anne Marsh Penton, 9-19, and "A School for 'Temporary Gentlemen': 'B' Company, No.2 Officer Cadet Battalion at Pembroke 1916-1919", by Charles Fair, 159-175. The Archivist, Lizzy Ennion-Smith kindly brought these to my attention. The two quotes come from 13 & 173.

[52] NLS Acc. 11627/37; Buchan, A., *Alastair Buchan*, 16-18; Buchan, J., *Memory-Hold-the-Door*, 255.

arrived. It was "a very nice weapon and it only cost £2. 5. (the usual price is £5)."[53] It must have been here that he really got to know "Steve" as they were in each other's company from April to November. During that time he was visited by Anna and his mother.[54]

In August he warned the latter that it was likely that they would go overseas soon, but was still unsure of the details. "I don't want to worry you, wee Mother, but it seems fairly likely this time. Of course it is good news for us, but not for you. But please don't worry about it."[55] This concern not to worry his family was a continuing theme right up to his last letter before being killed.

After six months there, and perhaps because he was good at training men, he unexpectedly remained behind when the battalion left in order to embark at Folkestone under Colonel Bunbury on the 20th September 1915. Having originally been *en route* for France, they then went on to Salonika under Colonel Buchanan in November. Had he gone with them his future life would have been very different, and he sensed the rebuff very keenly. "One feels a bit rotten when everybody is going away and one's men are going." They wanted a photograph taken with him.

He hoped that this would be possible when they

---

[53] Alastair to mother, RSF paper, n. d., JB Story Archive.

[54] Buchan, A., *Unforgettable*, 131.

[55] Alastair to mother, n. d. but presumably Sutton Veny, August 1915 from the context. JB Story Archive.

15. Alastair, with his training platoon
at Sutton Veny

returned from leave, and it is likely to be the one reproduced here. Though it is not titled in any way, we see Alastair immediately recognisable as the officer seated in the middle with his Sam Browne belt and cuffs of rank. [56]

Expecting a move near home, he wrote:[57]

The adjutant says that we leave for Stobs [the military training camp at Hawick] on 28th of next

---

[56] Buchan and Stewart, *Scots Fusiliers*, 338; Buchan, A., *Alastair Buchan*, 18. NLS Acc.11627/37, Letter to mother, n.d., but August 1915 from context.

[57] See articles about Stobs on the internet. After the camp closed in the 1950s, a young Jim Clark rallied there. Letter to mother n.d., in context about the time of her birthday, and a date in late August 1915 would fit. NLS Acc.11627/37.

month [September 1915]. It will be sad leaving here [Sutton Veny]. I have had the whole business of looking after my platoon for the last four months, and I like the men and I think they like me. It is beastly doing all that work and then not having the privilege of commanding them in the field. If ever I do go out it will be in command of a draft of men I do not know. I suppose it is useful work that we are doing but people do not understand that and wonder why we do not go out with the battalion while others who have only joined for a short time go out at once.

"Steve" may have felt the same. From Stobs Alastair wrote, probably in October, that they were marking time now, waiting to "carry on".

There is a horrid rumour that on the 9th we are going to Richmond, Yorks at an early date [the Army Garrison at Catterick was known as Richmond camp until 1915] – disquieting news for at least Stobs is near home. I am looking forward with much disquietude to spending another winter in England. One feels such a prize ass – nearly 12 months service and not a thing done as far as fighting is concerned.[58]

A sudden change of posting for Alastair was probably

---

[58] Letter to mother, embossed RSF paper, n.d. but "nearly 12 months service" would make it before the end of October 1915. NLS 11627/37; Buchan, A., *Alastair Buchan*, 19.

16. Alastair in England

prompted by the terrible Scottish losses in the Battle of Loos (25th September to 8th October) and the sudden urgent need for both officers and men as reinforcements.

Soon after this "Steve" went to France a week earlier than Alastair, though to the same regiment, the Royal Scots Fusiliers. However, each Brigade of four battalions had its own independent Trench Mortar Battery to which "Steve" was seconded. They then lost sight of each other, perhaps because he was originally posted to the 7th Battalion RSF while Alastair was serving with the 6th. These reasons would explain why they did not meet again for nearly a year, as we shall discover. [59] By that time the two battalions had been merged into the 6/7th RSF.

---

[59] Buchan, A., *Alastair Buchan*, 19. Though still with the mortars, "Steve" was officially in the 6/7 RSF when he died (CWGC inscription).

CHAPTER SIX

HIS FIRST WOUND AND RECUPERATION

Finally fulfilling his pressing desire, Alastair arrived
in France in December 1915, and joined the greatly
depleted Sixth (Service) Battalion, Royal Scots
Fusiliers. This had been formed on the outbreak of
War, and was part of the 27th Brigade, of the 9th
(Scottish) Division under Major-General William
Furse. It arrived in France in May 1915 in time to take
part in the Battle of Loos (September-October),
fighting gallantly but losing at least two-thirds of its
officers and half its other ranks in casualties. Despite
being so understrength it remained in the front line of
the Ypres Salient in the vicinity of Sanctuary Wood
and Maple Copse right until the 15th December. Four
days before the weather was so wet that the trenches
were collapsing.[60] Then it was sent by rail to recover
in reserve billets in the vicinity of Baillieul just over
the French border. Alastair will have joined it about
this time, and he may have been briefly exposed to
trench warfare at Ypres, depending on the actual date
he was put on the strength. Because of his "unquench-

---

[60] "6th RSF War Diary" 2nd & 6th December; Gilbert, M.,
Churchill, (2000 edition), says "late December", 342; for the
date of being relieved see "War Diary" 15th December.

able high spirits and radiant good nature", as well as his rude health, he became known there by his comrades affectionately as "the Glaxo baby" after the advert for dried milk, "Glaxo builds bonny babies." [61]

A good deal is known about life in the battalion during Alastair's time because Captain Dewar Gibb (1888-1974) wrote it up after the war. His account is greatly enhanced in a recent reprint which is supplemented by a large amount of explanatory text based upon contemporary sources which have only become available later. It also uses the War Diary of the 6th RSF and Gibb's own diary. On New Year's Day 1916 the battalion moved to the Meteren area in Northern France being billeted at Outersteene, with battalion headquarters nearby in the village of Moolenacker. [62]

There are other sources, particularly because Alastair's posting overlapped with that of a famous Commanding Officer whose life would be so well documented. Almost at once Colonel Dutton was replaced by Winston Churchill, and Alastair shared with him the same background experiences which are vividly recorded. The Cabinet minister had ceased to

---

[61] "6th RSF War Diary"; Soames, *Speaking*, 147. The 6th RSF War Diary is much less detailed than that of the 6/7th RSF in which Alastair later served. It does not give dates for of the arrival of officers, not even of the new Colonel in January. For "the Glaxo baby", see *Alastair Buchan*, 8.
[62] "6th RSF War Diary"; Soames, *Speaking*, 147.

be First Lord of the Admiralty after Gallipoli, re-activated his Territorial commission as a Major, and joined the British Expeditionary Force in France. After serving briefly with the Guards, he was offered this command, and it is often quoted that he wrote to his wife that "this regiment is pathetic." He did but, used out of context, it misinterprets.

His real meaning is important because he was speaking about people like Alastair. Before agreeing to take on the role he first

> made careful enquiries about the battalion. Like the rest of this Scottish division it fought with the greatest gallantry in the big battle [Loos] and was torn to pieces. More than half the men and three-quarters of the officers were shot & these terrible gaps have been filled up by recruits of good quality, and quite young inexperienced officers. In spite of its crippled condition the regiment has been for two months in the worst part of the line, but now they are resting & do not go in again until the 20th & then to an easier part. On these facts I think I shall take them.[63]

Alastair served the whole of the rest of his first brief period at the front under "the Right Honourable Colonel." The general feeling in anticipation was one

---

[63] Soames, *Speaking*, 145, Churchill to his wife, 1st January 1916.

of resentment that the man was being forced upon them.

Churchill arrived in time for lunch on 4th January,[64] and Alastair will have been one of those there who experienced the following uncomfortable initiation:

> Churchill didn't say a word: he went round the table staring each officer out of countenance. We had disliked the idea of Churchill being in command; now, having seen him, we disliked the idea even more. At the end of lunch, he made a short speech: 'Gentlemen, I am now your Commanding officer. Those who support me I shall look after. Those who go against me I will break. Good afternoon gentlemen.' Everyone was agreed that we were in for a pretty rotten time.[65]

---

[64] Buchan, A., *Alastair Buchan*, 20; Gibb, *At the Front*, 58. Churchill was in command of 6 RSF from 25th December 1915 to 6th May 1916, Buchan, *Scots Fusiliers*, 468. However, the commentary in Gibb says Churchill did not learn of his appointment to the battalion until "New Year's Day 1915 [sic]", Gibb, *At the Front*, 50. Both accounts err. Churchill's letter shows it was effective from New Year's Day 1916.

[65] Gibb, *At the Front*; and reminiscence by Major-General Sir Edmund Hakewill Smith in Gilbert, M., *Winston S. Churchill, Vol.III*, 632, quoted in Gibb, *At the Front*, 60. Soames, *Speaking*, 147, gives the joining date as the 5th January, but does not quote Churchill as saying this.

There was little space to train the men before going back to the front line on the 20th January, but Churchill entered upon the task with zest, determined that no part of the line would be in better hands. It was then that he wrote to his wife that "This regiment is 'pathetic.'" Officered by "small middle class Scotsman," they were "intelligent, very willing, but lacked military experience." However, he added that "the regiment is full of life

17. Lt.-Col. Churchill, commanding 6 RSF, with Major Sir Archibald Sinclair and Captain Gibb (seated), with 2/Lt. A. P. Skeil (standing behind in light coloured tie); photograph taken in March when Alastair had already gone home wounded.

and strength and I believe I shall be able to help them." Churchill saw potential in the raw material of both the men and the officers, being unlike his sometime Cabinet colleague, Lord Crawford, the premier earl of Scotland, who having spent fourteen months in the ranks, concluded that officers were not always heroes.

> This war is going to be won by the NCOs and men, not by the commissioned ranks. Eighteen months will develop a good soldier, a very passable NCO. But the period is too short to instil even the elements of leadership and control into the ordinary middle-class fellows who hold the commissions.... flabby, easy-going... young men brought up in affluence....[66]

This was not Churchill's experience of men like young Buchan and his friend "Old Skeil" (see below, 59ff.), nor was it true of Alastair's friend, Stevenson.

With his constant good humour, described elsewhere, Alastair did not need Churchill's injunction to them that "War is a game that is to be played with a smile. If you can't smile, grin."[67] Despite training them hard, Churchill soon completely won the hearts of his men through his generous understanding and

_____

[66] Quoted by Hugh Cecil in *The Spectator*, 12th April 2014 from *Crawford's Great War Diaries*, 206.; cf. Buchan's contrary view, 149-150.

[67] Quoted by Cecil, *The Spectator*, 91.

care, he took pride in them. Moreover, he was not an alien Englishman, but had been M.P. for Dundee since 1908 and had married the grand-daughter of a Scottish nobleman the previous year. Ten days before Alastair was wounded it was said that Churchill had "turned the battalion from moderate to 'd----- good.'"[68] Though often described as not having liked him, Buchan went out of his way to quote at length, in his *History* of the Regiment, Captain Gibb's glowing appreciation of his commander. They were engaged in no major battle during the few months under his command, but still suffered a hundred and thirty-eight killed and wounded. Without becoming casualties through face to face conflict, it is surprising that so

---

[68] Colonel 'Tom' Holland, R.A., of the 15th Division (afterwards Lieut.-General Sir Arthur Edward Aveling Holland, MP 1862-1927) to 'Mrs Winston', 18th February 1917. Gilbert, *Winston S. Churchill, Vol.III*, 674. Churchill would say that "it was in Scotland that I found the three best things in my life – my wife, my constituency and my regiment." Paul Cowan doubts the sincerity of the last comment in "Churchill in the Trenches" on his blog "Scottish Military Disasters" because he wore the uniform of the Oxfordshire Hussars in later life. Against the sceptics it should be said that the RSF was <u>his</u> regiment in the sense that it was the only one he ever commanded in war. As for the Hussars, he will have worn that uniform only on formal occasions in England, and it is hard to imagine that Winston ever had cause to possess RSF dress when he only served with them briefly in the trenches.

many died from random firing and accident, as well as those who succumbed from disease.[69]

In many ways Alastair was fortunate in his overseas posting. He soon found himself under a commander who quickly proved to be both efficient and compassionate.[70] He was in congenial company and, during the whole time he was there, in a pretty quiet part of the Front. There was no "going over the top" for it was "very unlikely to be the scene of an attack by either side", though there were excursions into No-Man's Land under cover of darkness.[71] The thousand yard section of trenches to be held was in much better condition than many elsewhere. They had

---

[69] Buchan and Stewart, *Scots Fusiliers*, 345-346: "At first the prospect frightened us, but those feelings did not survive the first week. We came to realise... his tremendous ability. He came to be looked on as really a possession... of which we were intensely proud. And much more, he became our friend." In return, Churchill wrote to his cousin, the Duke, on the 22nd January, three weeks after taking over: "The battalion has improved since I came & the utmost loyalty & wish to do right characterises everybody.... But think what the professional soldiers will have said of a battalion so composed and efficient": quoted in Gibb, *At the Front*, 89.

[70] When Churchill arrived, confidence was understandably low. "After a very brief period he accelerated the morale of the officers and men to an unbelievable degree. It was sheer personality. He had a unique approach which did wonders for us." Gibb, *At the Front*, 123-124, and for his compassion, 44, 71 et al.

[71] Ibid., 90 & 107.

"duck boards for the men to walk along, and drainage ditches had been dug. This meant that the soldiers could live and fight in dry conditions." Again, "the parapets were strong and bullet-proof and the dug-outs provided good shelter." Then in the trenches there were also "good communications, good wire, and minor conveniences."[72]

However, "rest" periods were spent only fifteen-hundred yards from the Front Line and still in as much danger from enemy artillery of all kinds, and the risk of gas attack. Churchill was also greatly concerned that command of the air had been lost to the enemy, for their planes flew overhead being virtually unchallenged.[73]

Alastair's time in the trenches during this first tour of duty was very limited. Having reached Ploegsteert (anglicised as "Plugstreet") on 20th January, the battalion first entered the trenches for only two days, from the 27th to the 29th January, to accustom them to the front line. Thereafter, the regular pattern of six days in trenches, alternating with six days in "rest", was followed.[74] The actual time that he spent there can be gleaned from the War Diary. His first period of six days lasted from the 1st - 6th February, followed by the second from the 13th - 18th. The third began on the 25th but was terminated on the

---

[72] Gibb, *At the Front*, 83 & 89.

[73] Ibid., 105 & 136.

[74] Ibid., 96 & 103.

evening of the following day, as we shall see. He may have been in the trenches briefly near Ypres in early December, but otherwise his total service in the front line, rather than in "rest" or training, was only sixteen days before returning home wounded.

Once in France, Alastair maintained his liking for men of all ranks. He formed a "great admiration" for "a decent wee lad" in his platoon. Knowing that his officer's dug-out was draughty, he filled in between the sand-bags and made a shutter for the window, as well as being equally helpful in action. He volunteered for a wiring party under Alastair, "not a very pleasant job owing to the M.G. fire."

> There are two corporals in my company that I love. They are called Dobson and Hamilton and have been friends from the beginning. They are both wonderful and don't know what fear is – a thing which a timid man like myself marvels at. Also they have a marvellous sense of direction, and are kindly disposed towards the weaker sex (that's me again). They form my bodyguard, and every time I fall into a shell-hole or dodge a crump you can hear them shout, "Are ye hurt, Mr Buchan?" They both wear the Military Medal.

There was "a splendid Sergeant" in his platoon who was "an old Gallowgate policeman."

Alastair quickly found a soul mate in "Old Skeil", "a most amusing man.... the kindest-hearted and most conscientious… I ever struck", who "never grouses."[75] Examples given in letters included Skeil waking them up shouting "The huns are only a hundred yards off!" which, "although it sounds startling at first, is true." Asked one night to be woken at 11 p.m. to go round his wiring parties, Skeil went out himself, "though he loathes the whole job", giving his young friend two hours more sleep.[76]

After active service of little more than two months, on the 26th February Alastair received a slight wound in the right thigh from friendly fire, and was admitted to the 1 Red Cross Hospital, Letouquet, two days later.[77] The circumstances of this were that

> The day after the battalion had returned into the front line, there was a burst of artillery activity, as the War Diary reveals: 'At 11.30 pm our guns fired in the trenches opposite T103-112 with 20 rounds deliberate and 20 rapid. At the same time

---

[75] Buchan, A. *Alastair Buchan*, 22-24; forming his bodyguard is interesting. Churchill had said that every officer should be watched over by his batman and another, but this had proved impossible in practice. Gibb, *At the Front*, 99. The two corporals seem to have effected it voluntarily. Later Buchan has a fictional character, Geordie Hamilton, who had supposedly been a soldier in the RSF. He becomes Hannay's batman in *Mr Stanfast*.

[76] Buchan, A., *Alastair Buchan*, 23-24. Illust.18 was copied from original photographs possessed by local villagers.

[77] On the 1st March the Peebles family received a telegram to inform them, NLS 11627/37.

18. An artistic impression in stone of the battered Church, & well-constructed trenches that Alastair will often have looked out on in "Plugstreet"

the enemy's line was bombarded with trench mortars & rifle grenades & and companies fired 50 rounds rapid. Cease fire was at 11.40 pm. The enemy retaliated with a few 7.7cms which did no damage. Some of our shells burst short on the left (T110) wounding 4 men and killing two. 2nd Lieut. A. E. Buchan was slightly wounded.'[78]

Nevertheless, he was repatriated, and stayed "at Queensferry all that summer." A slight wound would be unlikely to keep him in hospital for months, and there happened to be the 9th (Reserve) Battalion of his

---

[78] Gibb, *At the Front*, 137-138.

Regiment at North Queensferry. He was declared fit for "general service" on 4th May and joined them on the 19th. Until October, he was there as a training officer once again, as at Sutton Veny.[79] Sometime earlier, Alastair had been able to visit his eldest brother's family who were in London. This photograph could also have the caption "Lieutenant, two brothers, two Colonels, father & son."

19. Alastair as a favourite uncle

Now, during the few months at North Queensferry, Alastair had the opportunity of seeing more of his family in Peebles, since he quite often got leave, coming "prancing home, so sun-burnt and

---

[79] Buchan, A., *Alastair Buchan*, 20; National Archives WO 339/26528; Buchan, A. *Unforgettable*, 146.

jolly."[80] Anna tells us that "All children loved Alastair." "He was so gentle with the tiny ones and such a splendid player." She recounts what happened one sunny afternoon on his last visit to Broughton in the summer of 1916. Together she and Alastair came upon Buchan's two young children, sitting by the burn-side with their Nannie. The younger was known as "Mr John", and the older, Alice, had said that "there is no one I love like my Uncle As", but she is not recorded as taking part in the incident which followed.[81]

There were some natural trenches in the field and we had a battle – Alastair and Mr John (British) [their nephew aged five] against Nannie and me (German). Milly and Billy Fish watched the fray, and Mr John said, 'They are the Kaiser and the Crown Prince.' It was a glorious battle, and Nannie and I were hopelessly routed. I can see Alastair in his grey tweed suit leaping with Mr John in his arms, and shouting as light-hearted and care-free as if the world held nothing more serious than this mimic warfare. In another month he was back in the real trenches. Every day after that Mr John led me to the field and suggested coaxingly that we might have another

---

[80] Buchan, A., *Alastair Buchan*, 20.
[81] Ibid., 12-13. "Uncle As" was his nickname used by Buchan's children.

battle. But we never did. How could we when the one who made playing real was away?

Endnote on Churchill and Scotland (see above, 50)

We have seen that Churchill would say that "it was in Scotland that I found the three best things in my life – my wife, my constituency, and my regiment" (see above 50, note 68). Now what of this seat in Parliament? He was a Liberal M.P. for Dundee (1908-1922), a member of the Cabinet at the early age of thirty-three, then Home Sectary 1910-1911, First Lord of The Admiralty 1911-1915, Minister of Munitions 1917-1918, Secretary of State for War & Air, 1919-1921, and for the Colonies until he lost his seat in 1922. As early as 1912 he advocated Home Rule for Scotland. In a speech in Dundee he proposed "a federal system in the United Kingdom in which Scotland, Ireland, and if necessary parts of England, could have separate legislative and parliamentary institutions." (*The National*, 5th July 2016) His "service on the Western Front was often to bring him much support." For example, there is a letter in the press from Bandmaster Robertson, before his re-election in 1917. He reports on the views of the 6th RSF that Churchill was "one of the very best" who "would do everything for us, and we would do anything for him." (Gibb, 185-186).

Endnote on Officers (see above, 49)

Because of lack of space, this has been moved to 64.

CHAPTER SEVEN

"OLD SKEIL"

Alastair says that "Old Skeil" was senior to the rest of us. Born on 7th August 1882 in Coatbridge, Alexander Patrick Skeil was twelve years older when they met as fellow Second Lieutenants in France at the end of 1915.

20. "Old Skeil"

The son of a cashier he, too, had graduated from the University of Glasgow but later than usual, in 1907, and had not overlapped with Alastair. He became a teacher at Langloan Primary School in his home town.[82] He did not enlist until 1915. Having been commissioned, he met Alastair in the December. Wounded in the following April, he was sent to hospital in Dublin, being there during the Easter Rising (24th – 29th April 1916).[83]

When Alastair returned to France in October 1916, he found him long returned, still a temporary Second Lieutenant but acting locally as a Captain. During the Battle of the Somme which ended in November, Skeil had won the Military Cross, though his award was not gazetted until the 29th December 1916. He was very modest about this. Alastair recounted that he was "wearing the ribbon of his M.C. in his pocket. I can see we shall have to force him to put it up." Thereafter, his military career took off. Once having taken over command of B Company, to Alastair's great delight he was placed under him. Colonel Gordon rated him as "a most excellent fellow." Before Easter 1917 he was temporarily rested, with Alastair taking over the Company (four times more troops than were usually led by a Lieutenant in a platoon). Writing in his last letter home Alastair said that, as great friends, they "bade each other a tearful farewell." He was seriously wounded in the right arm on 16th April. This did not affect his

---

[82] Lang, *Roll of Honour*; Lindsay, *Coatbridge*, 50.

[83] Personal communication from Alasdair Skeil (grandson), 9th September 2019.

ability to continue to be the key bowler in his local cricket team after the war.[84]

Having recovered, Skeil would later become Lieutenant-Colonel commanding the 2/10th Royal Scots fighting from Archangel under Buchan's friend, Edmund Ironside from 1918-1919. His battalion was a motley crew of officers being rested from France, like himself, and men who, after the weaker had been weeded out, were at least medically B1 (fit for garrison duty), with others from anywhere who made up the strength to a thousand. In acquitting itself well, the battalion suffered more casualties than any other. For this activity he was created a Companion of the Distinguished Service Order on 1st February 1919. This was especially for actions the previous autumn on the Dvina river, including the epic

> forest-march [which] was a feat of amazing endurance, and fortitude and would certainly have resulted in the utter destruction of the force

---

[84] On the ribbon: Alastair to Walter, RSF, 20 January 1917. NLS Acc. 11627/37; Skeil did not escape popular recognition for long. On his next visit to Coatbridge, the Council publicly presented him with an illuminated address of congratulation. *Coatbridge Leader*, 23rd June 1917. For "excellent fellow", Gordon, to Buchan, 6/7 RSF, 29 December 1917, NLS, ibid. For Colonel Gordon see below, 71ff.; "great friends", Buchan, A., *Alastair Buchan*, 33-34. For his wound, see *Coatbridge Express*, 18th April 1917; Roll of Honour, *Glasgow Evening Times*, January – April 1917.

but for the resolution of the men and the quality of the leader. They so surprised the Bolsheviks that they fled from the town which Skeil had gone to attack.

Buchan recruited him for *The Long Road to Victory*, and his article on, "The River Column in North Russia August 1918-July 1919", ends with: "our experiences none of us would have cared to miss, but none would care to repeat." [85] His grandson relates that "he stayed good friends with the Buchan family; there is a full set of John's books, signed by John, but unfortunately Pickfords mislaid them whilst my parents were in Singapore (where I was born)".[86]

Returning to Coatbridge in 1919, he continued at Langloan School, and in playing cricket for the local Drumpellier Cricket Club first XI. In the summer of 1923 he "captained and led the team with conspicuous success." In August 1925 he married into the Bell whisky family, and had a son who was born there. He continued in his home town into the mid-thirties, for he was acting as President of the British Legion branch

---

[85] Wright, *Churchill's Secret War*, 149; Ewing, *The Royal Scots*, 745-747; Skeil's somewhat ramblingly detailed account, presumably from a diary, is in Buchan, *Long Road*, 297-332. Being a professional soldier, Ewing was in a good position to give the commendation about Skeil and his men. Buchan, *Long Road*, 332.

[86] Personal communication from Alasdair Skeil, 9th September 2019.

and, like Buchan was "an elder of the Kirk."[87] Both being ordained as such, they may have met at the General Assembly. In 1938 he moved to Wishaw where he was the "highly-esteemed and popular headmaster" of Newmains Primary and Junior Secondary School.[88] "He served again with Field Marshal Lord Ironside at the start of WW2 in the Home Guard."[89] He retired in 1947, and moved briefly to Galashiels, before settling in St Andrews, where he died on 8th February 1959, but was buried in Coatbridge.[90]

My reading of Skeil may be wrong, but from what little I have pieced together he seems to have been a small town boy who wished for little more. Perhaps because he had to save to keep himself, five years later than most he made a dash to Glasgow to get his degree. Thereafter he was content to live out his life in North Lanarkshire. His sole ambition, apparently, was to teach in a primary school, and in that vocation he was content to be fulfilled despite

---

[87] *Coatbridge Advertiser*, 6th October 1923; *Coatbridge Leader*, 8th August 1925; *Coatbridge Express*, 26th September 1934; personal communication from Alasdair Skeil, 9th September 2019. Having exhausted all avenues in searching for a newspaper obituary for Skeil, I wonder whether he left instructions that there was not to be one.

[88] *Wishaw Press*, 4th July 1947.

[89] Personal communication from Alasdair Skeil, 9th September 2019.

[90] *Glasgow Herald*, 11th February 1959.

marrying into a presumably wealthier family than might have been expected. In less than five untypical and extraordinary years he had a distinguished military career despite apparently loathing the whole business. Success did not turn his head, but he simply retired to his roots and "stuck to his last". Unless he gained unsung promotion in Coatbridge, it was late in his career before he obtained a headship elsewhere. What real fame he achieved he did not seek, and apart perhaps from on the cricket field, what glory he attained was thrust upon him. Some will judge this to have been as a Christian gentleman, and to his greater honour. His taking young Buchan under his wing, was certainly to the considerable benefit of both.

Endnote on Officers (see above, 49)

The monument at Holborn Bar to my father's fusilier regiment is to 22,000 men who died. On the heroics, or otherwise, of officers, he told me that he, and his men, sometimes felt abandoned by superiors who had been "killed or ridden off the field." This criticism might have been partly occasioned as gallantry awards were only given on the recommendation of a superior officer. Military Crosses (ribbons), it was said "came up with the rations", as though they had not been earned, which was a bit hard. Unlike campaign medals, the receiving of a deserved order or gallantry award, and how it was bestowed, was less certain whatever your rank. Without a D.S.O., Colonel Gordon was under-decorated for what he did well for so long, and that would take precedence over his O.B.E.

CHAPTER EIGHT

RETURNING TO THE FRONT

In the autumn of 1916 Alastair was posted back to France, and his telegram reached Peebles on 29th October saying that he had arrived safely.[91] When he rejoined the battalion on the 4th November, he found it merged into the 6/7 RSF, and commanded by Major Thomas Smith (1868-1917), deputising for Colonel Edward Ian Drumearn Gordon (1877-1942) who did not return from leave in England until the 19th. [92] Posted to B Company, under Skeil who was already a Captain, they were at Franvillers when five days later Haig came to inspect them, and reported favourably.[93] That approval showed Smith's competence as well as

---

[91] Buchan, A , *Alastair Buchan*, 21.

[92] The battalions were merged in May and Gordon took over on 25th June 1916, having previously been a Deputy Assistant Adjutant and Quartermaster General for which he had just been mentioned in despatches. Details of Gordon's career can be gleaned from the *London Gazette*. Two of his Christian names being Edward and Drumearn, seem to indicate that the family were related to Edward Gordon, who became Lord Gordon of Drumearn (1814-1879). In fact, his mother was the peer's daughter, and her husband's second cousin; *Who Was Who*; CWGC record; Bullock, *Military Family*.

[93] "War Diary", 4th, 9th, & 24th November.

Gordon's effectiveness as a commander. Only in late June 1916 had he taken over the challenging task of merging into one, as the 6/7 RSF, two battalions which were both so depleted that "there were no longer enough in either to form two effective fighting units." Moreover, the 6th was fresh from mourning the personal loss of Churchill as their commander.[94]

Gordon's ability to integrate the two battalions is shown by Alastair, once loyal to the distinguished predecessor. He soon become very happy under his new superiors, readily transferring his devotion and in January he wrote to Walter that "I have never been in a battalion where it was so pleasant to serve under both the C.O. and the Major [Smith]."[95] Ironically Smith was killed three days after this was written. Buchan will have admired the upwardly mobile Scottish families from which both men came. Though Gordon now belonged to the historic officer class, his great-grandfather had been no more than a tacksman (tenant farmer) in Griamachary, parish of Kildonan, on the island of Arran. Smith was a self-made man, like Gordon's great-uncle, who had served as a Sergeant

---

[94] Gilbert, *Winston S. Churchill*, Vol.III, 758-760.

[95] Alastair to Walter, 20th January 1917, NLS Acc.11627/37. Gordon was in command of the newly combined 6/7 RSF from 25th June 1916, taking the battalion through the battle of the Somme, and right on to the beginning of 1918: Buchan, *Scots Fusiliers*, 346-347 & 468. The photograph of Smith (71) is from *The Illustrated London News*, 27th February 1917, 238.

*21. Gordon as a
young officer after the
South African War*

for some years before getting a commission.[96] The
Buchans will have liked them both for these different
reasons, but more because they were gallant and
caring.

First there is Smith. It is difficult to research
someone with only two names, both borne by many
others. In *The Illustrated London News* for the 24th
February 1917, page 238, there is an *In Memoriam*
photograph captioned

[96] Bullock, *Military Family*, 6. Curiously enough he retired to
the Cape, as Gordon would do.

Major Thomas Smith, DCM (South Africa). R. Scots Fusiliers. Son of the late Alexander Smith, Stonehouse.

It is important to note that there were not two such Major T. Smiths in the RSF who were killed in 1917.[97] Stonehouse, in Lanarkshire, is a small village. It wasn't difficult to discover that an illiterate colliery worker, Alexander Smith, and his wife Isabella had a son called Thomas born in June 1868. This was in a country where basic primary education was supposed to have been universal from the Reformation onwards. At the 1871 Census, Thomas was then the youngest of seven children, his two oldest brothers already working in the mines.[98] As he grew to manhood, he had the initiative to escape from all that at the earliest opportunity. On, or very near, his sixteenth birthday in June 1884 he enlisted as a boy soldier in the ranks of the Gordon Highlanders. Two years later he began to serve as a private in that regiment.

In 1895, already a Sergeant (service number 1480), he received the India General Service medal for fighting frontier wars, adding two clasps for Waziristan and another two years later for taking part in the storming of the Dargai Heights in Malakand as a Colour-Sergeant. In the same year his son Alexander

---

[97] Buchan & Stewart, *Scots Fusiliers*, 409.
[98] Birth, and 1871 Census details from the National Records of Scotland.

Hamilton, was born, and six weeks later the mother, Helen, died in Rawalpindi at the age of twenty-three. He was transferred in March 1899 to the London Scottish as Sergeant-Major.

With the outbreak of the South African War Smith was transferred into the City of London Imperial Volunteers in the same rank. For the first seven months he was besieged in Mafeking. Then in September 1901 he was awarded the Distinguished Conduct Medal, and in 1902 the Coronation Medal as a member of the parade. Thereafter he continued in the army as a Sergeant-Major instructor with London Volunteer Battalions including the Middlesex Volunteer Rifle Company, probably until 1908 when the Territorial Force was created. Then he retired and, having eighteen years of exemplary service, he had been awarded his Army Long Service and Good Conduct Medal in 1905.

At some time having remarried, Smith was living in Sussex Square "engaged in the dressmaking business." During these years, he had the satisfaction of seeing his son well-educated at Margate Grammar School and then at Christ's Hospital (Blue Coat). From there he entered upon a good career to become a ship's officer, having joined the *Mersey*, a training ship owned by White Star, as a cadet in 1912.

When war broke out in 1914, Smith was either recalled to the colours or volunteered. He was immediately commissioned (September). In a

promotion sometimes give to well-regarded senior
N.C.O.s he became an honorary Second-Lieutenant
(Quartermaster). Because of his past battle experience
he was promoted Captain on the 27th January 1915,
and appointed Adjutant of the 9th (Service) Battalion
of The Gordon Highlanders. Originally a pioneer unit,
they crossed to Boulogne on the 8th July in time to
take part in the Battle of Loos. [99]

After the terrible losses suffered there by the 9th
Division various units were in need of re-organisation.
When Churchill and Sinclair left the 6th Royal Scots
Fusiliers in the Spring of 1916 it was an appropriate
time to amalgamate them with the 7th battalion. Smith
was promoted and drafted in as second in command to
Colonel Gordon, deputising during his absences. He
must have been the most decorated, and most
experienced in war of the officers in the battalion;
possibly the oldest. By the time Alastair knew him he
was long remarried and living in Bayswater.

It is strange pity that he is so shrouded in
mystery on his grave. There is only the normal initial
letter "T." for his Christian name; no mention of his
family or of his long-standing service in The Gordon
Highlanders; no D.C.M. (see below Endnote on 81);
he was only attached to the Royal Scots Fusiliers, with
even his battalion wrongly given as the former 6th,
when it should be updated to the 6/7th; and there is no

---

[99] Information in these paragraphs is gleaned from the internet;
Army Lists, and The Gordon Highlanders Museum, Aberdeen.

22. Major Thomas Smith, D.C.M.

personal epitaph, but only a standard formal one. It is almost as though no more accurate details were known. He seems modestly elusive on his memorial.

There is more to say about Gordon. Elsewhere, Alastair reaffirmed that "it is a pleasure to work under Col. Gordon. He is one of the finest men I ever met and he has been awfully kind to me. I would hate to disappoint him."[100] He did not, as we shall soon see below. His father, General Sir John Gordon, GCB, was twin brother to General Sir Thomas Gordon, and Lord Gordon of Drumearn and Surgeon-General Huntly Gordon were their cousins. Educated at

---

[100] Buchan, A, *Alastair Buchan*, 35.

Wellington,[101] he served in the South African War, taking part in a number of engagements including the long delayed Relief of Ladysmith. Now in France, for fully two years he led the 6/7th and then the first battalion of the RSF, almost twice as long a period as any other Commanding Officer in the regiment, but his only decoration was a second mention in despatches in December 1917.

However, it was not until the last of the wartime lists, in the Birthday Honours 1919, that he was given some further recognition with the awarded of an O.B.E., before finally being promoted substantive Lieut.-Colonel and going onto retired pay in that July. Buchan clearly respected Gordon who was two years younger, and singled him out for mention in his *History*. Deneys Reitz, a former Boer Commando, served under him after Alastair's death and commanded the first battalion for a couple of months as the war ended. He wrote that Gordon "seemed to be made of whip-cord and said he was not tired" and "was to all intents and purposes a South African" and married to one, for owning "a farm in the Western Cape...he was going to retire there if he survived...."

---

[101] *Wellington College Register 1859-1896*, 236. He entered for the Michaelmas Term 1891. However, there was a suspected diphtheria out break and the school was sent home at the beginning of December. He did not return. Caroline Jones, Archivist, 1st October 2019. I have not established whether he went to another school or to a tutor. Sandhurst does no know.

He did.[102] Later, like his brother, John, he died in service, and lies in a Commonwealth War Grave in Cape Town (Maitland) Cemetery. Despite being past retirement age, he had found some way to serve, and died in 1942 as a Lieutenant-Colonel in the South African Staff Corps. It was a fitting end to one hundred and forty years of service by the family. He married Maude, daughter of A. C. M. Blackman, also South African, in 1915, and twin sons joined the British army in 1946.

In such a class structured society in which Smith had long served in the ranks, he is a wonderful example of upward mobility. The wartime opportunities of being "a temporary gentleman" brought him unexpectedly into working intimately

---

[102] For the information in this paragraph see Buchan and Stewart, *Scots Fusiliers*, 452. Reitz, D., *Adrift on the Open Veldt*. 160. He does not say that he served under Gordon twice, first in 1917, before being severely wounded at the end of that year, and again in 1918. Reitz joined the 6/7 RSF near Arras in April 1917 when commanded by "Colonel de Haviland" who was a Major acting for Gordon, having replaced Smith as 2i/c. For Col. Gordon, see CWGC record. This accords with the way some have imagined Buchan's "musketeers" would have behaved had they fictionally still been alive in 1939, Buchan, A., *Unforgettable*, 143. Captain John Frederick Strathearn Gordon, Cameronians (Scottish Rifles), died of wounds on 19th November 1914, buried at Poperinge in Belgium (CWGC). As a result of my correspondence, Edward Gordon's name has been added to the SNWM to join his brother, *e-mail* from Mary-Clare Macfarlane, Assistant Secretary, 11 June 2020.

together with a General's son, who had graduated from the Staff College and had all the advantages. From his father's illiterate background, he had risen to commanding, albeit for short spells, hundreds of men in battle. Alastair's testimony to them working together in such harmony is a considerable tribute to the characters of both men. Had Smith survived the war, it is doubtful that the army would have had much space for a fifty-year-old major or colonel with such a background. He would have reverted to the retired list and at least Mrs Gertrude Smith had a widow's pension.

Alastair's returned to the trenches in November 1916 in very different circumstances than at Ploegsteert, and the battalion had experienced "tempestuous gales and drenching rains" in the previous month. They were coming out of holding the line at Le Sars, Arras, in what were "no more than a string of shell holes linked up by shallow trenches." Alastair was initially fortunate because on the day after he arrived in such conditions the battalion was then "rested" in the village of Franvillers. This was on the 5th November, and Buchan was not far off at G.H.Q. [103] It must have been on the same day that he drove out there at once only to be told that Alastair was bringing in the last lot of men from the trenches – a very weary, foot-sore lot they were.

---

[103] Buchan, A., *Alastair Buchan*, 27-28; the locations are taken from the daily 6/7 RSF daily "War Diary".

John… saw Alastair before Alastair saw him. He told us later that as he watched him striding along at the head of his men a pang went through his heart. It seemed to him that this little brother of his was too shining-eyed, too much all that was innocent and young and brave to win through.

Of course, the men had been manning the inadequate trenches for weeks, whereas Alastair was newly returned from home. B Company took up quarters in the village in King Street and spent the rest of the month training with the battalion in the surrounding area, so that the conditions were better. It was around this time that he wrote, [104]

we are trying to light a fire [but]… the fuel is damp. Perhaps it won't go because we are using the *British Weekly* as paper. Browning suggests something inflammatory like *John Bull*, and someone else *Greenmantle*, [Buchan's novel, which had only just been published.]

Early in December they moved to Albert, and on the 19th December Alastair led the advanced party which took over the camp at Shelter Woods prior to manning the Le Sars trenches again. Christmas approached, and he anticipated spending it somewhat

---

[104] Buchan and Stewart, *Scots Fusiliers*, 360 & 361; Buchan, A., *Alastair Buchan*, 24; *Greenmantle* was published in book form on 26th October 1916, Hillier, *First Editions*, 50.

in an

early Christian manner – not in mirth and feasting but in fasting. I expect the mirth will be there too… We are living in a muddy little dug-out, which smells 'orful [sic], but it is quite warm and comfortable.

In fact, he "spent Christmas taking a working-party up the line. We got shelled, sniped, and met the Brigadier [F. W. H. Walshe] – I don't know which was worst!" On the last day of 1916 the battalion was pulled back in reserve to Shelter Woods South Camp, so that "Coming out [of the trenches] was a beastly business as our packs were rather heavy and I fell into almost

*23. What Alastair longed for – a Field
Kitchen on the Somme, November 1917*

every shell-hole there was." Very fed up, he enquired for rations, though none had come yet, but there was a letter from Anna which began, "We have just finished a large dinner and are sitting beside a very large fire, this is a very comfortable hotel." Alastair commented that, "I read it out to a crowd of miserables and we fairly roared with laughter." [105]

It was there, on the following day that Buchan, having been recalled to London to become Director of Information, arrived to say farewell. He was accompanied by his old Oxford friend, Sandy Gillon.

24. Muddy Conditions around Le Sars

The Scots Fusiliers had just had a very bad time in the Le Sars area, and "Alastair's rosy face and broad smile struck Gillon as being about the cheeriest sight

---

[105] "War Diary"; Buchan, A., *Alastair Buchan*, 25-26.

he had seen at the Front". Together "they had a great New Year's dinner, with the pipes playing, and everyone in great form."

Obviously, the officers were faring better than the men, for the youngest brother wrote cheerfully to Walter that

> This is a lovely chateau and the country round about is very pretty.... It is rather a funny thing that the owner of this chateau whose name is the same as the village with a 'de' added on is a private serving in the French army! [106]

During this time Alastair had the delight of renewing his friendship with "Steve". Having been together training with the Royal Scots Fusiliers, the two found themselves again in the same vicinity only when Alastair arrived in France for the second time. They enjoyed a lot of contact over the next three months until he was killed by a high explosive shell on 28th January 1917 near the ruins of the village of Le Sars astride the Albert-Bapaume road, two days after his twenty-second birthday. Having been promoted Lieutenant, and recently mentioned-in-despatches, he had evidently been taking part in preparations for the raid on the Butte de Warlencourt.

---

[106] Alastair to Walter, 20th January 1917: NLS Acc.11627/37. Evidently, a willingness to serve in any capacity was not limited to Britain.

Alastair was one of those who buried him in Peake Wood Cemetery, Fricourt.

As a little boy Alastair hated sad things and would always ask of a book, "Does anyone die?" Nevertheless, he could not resist *Morte d'Arthur* as a bed-time story, weeping and howling with rage at the beauty of the poetry and himself for listening.[107] Now death was an ever-present reality and often random. It could strike when least expected. As Churchill was to observe, it had become hardly noticed. On one occasion when on parade a bomb in a soldier's pouch exploded, killing him and wounding nine comrades. On another, there was a field Court Martial into how a man had got his injuries. One new subaltern was killed two days after arriving. Then on the 23rd January Major Smith, of whom Alastair thought highly, was temporarily in command again when Gordon was absent. He took a subaltern with him and set out on a routine visit to some men in the front line. There, both officers were hit by the explosion of a whizz-bang,[108] and wounded, Smith fatally.

In the same month Alastair was gazetted acting

---

[107] *Alastair Buchan*, 8-9; for the burial of "Steve", ibid., 20.

[108] A whizz-bang was "a small-calibre shell travelling at such a high velocity that the sound of its flight was heard only an instant, if at all, before the sound of its explosion." Smith is buried at Peake Wood Cemetery, Fricourt, with Alastair's friend Stevenson, killed five days later. Buchan and Stewart, *Scots Fusiliers*, mentions him only in passing, 359 & 409.

Lieutenant, because Gordon had already promoted him "specially over the heads of others not because he was John Buchan's brother but because he was Alastair Buchan, a capable officer." That was the Colonel's view, but whether it was as easy for Alastair is questionable. Others do not take readily to having their equals promoted above them and, as yet, he really had very little experience of trench warfare, his total service in France being little more than four months, though he had spent many more in training men at home. Nevertheless, he must have coped well, for we shall see that he kept his commander's high regard of him as a soldier and, still more impressively, the respect of his peers. During the very bad and difficult winter, Alastair's "letters were uniformly cheerful." After having

> a trying forty-eight hours in the front trenches – up to the waist in liquid mud, and no food but a dry biscuit… he always liked to finish with, 'One can stand anything for forty-eight hours.'

This was typical of the cheery and positive attitude in his letters home that Alastair always attempted to convey, in the futile hope of preventing them from worrying about him at the front. "Only for home service" his mother had forlornly begged when he volunteered. "Hers was the old cry, '*Simeon* [William?] *is not, Joseph* [Violet?] *is not, wilt thou take Benjamin also?*' But this Benjamin was so willing to go."[109] Her hopes must have risen when for a whole year he was still at home, and for two years he was only abroad for three months.

Endnote on Major Smith's D.C.M.

When photographed Smith is wearing a single row of five ribbons (see above, 71), but I have shown that he had been awarded six medals. Professor Sim (see above, xi) tells me that recipients of the Coronation Medal often did not put it up. Moreover, those commissioned from the ranks might not display medal ribbons for decorations awarded to enlisted men. Either explanation would explain only five worn.

---

[109] "War Diary", 27th February refers to *The London Gazette*, 3rd January, when Skeil "(acting Captain whilst commanding a Company)" is also listed, so that Gordon must have promoted Alastair (and three others, perhaps one for each of the four companies) "acting" earlier in the field; "University of Glasgow Story"; *Alastair Buchan*, 24. Gordon's comment, ibid., 36; ibid. 27-29; for "home service" *Unforgettable*, 142.

CHAPTER NINE

HIS LAST DAYS AND DEATH

Alastair's second period of active service was spent in and around the Le Sars section of the line. He slept at places on the map of his last fight, including more than once at Duisans, where he would be buried.[110] His leave was due in March, but on being moved to Arras he knew that it had gone "very far West."[111] Nevertheless, during the last two weeks of March, "we have had a fine rest" and on Sunday, 1st April "there was no Presbyterian, so I went to attend the English Church Service, which was nice and quiet and simple. We read a most appropriate psalm [91] about the terrors by night, etc." That was to be his last peaceful time. The next day they "expected to move" and

> there may be a stoppage of letters for a few days, but don't worry.... Things may be happening soon, but don't worry about me. I was just thinking last night what a good time I have had

---

[110] 6/7th RSF "War Diary".

[111] Buchan, A., *Alastair Buchan*, 29; there may be a misprint in Buchan and Stewart, *Scots Fusiliers*, 373-374 implies that two platoons of B Company, 6/7 RSF were engaged in raiding parties on 22nd March and 7th April, losing two officers. There is no record of such activity or losses in the "War Diary."

all round and what a lot of happiness I have had. Even the sad bits are a comfort now.[112]

During "the terrible cannonade" (4th-8th April) before the battle, despite the military camaraderie he remained devoted to his family, and wrote home about family matters, sending a cheque for Anna's birthday written in pencil. Concerned about his mother's health he added, "You know you mean home, and the day doesn't seem complete without a letter from you." He could see the humour in being able to "dine in comfort in a restaurant."[113] Enclosing a photograph with fellow officers, Anna remarked that "You can't help smiling back when you look at it – there is such a broad, cheery grin on his face. Across the back he put,

"*Toujours* smiley face."

On Good Friday, 6th April, he attended what would be his last Church parade. The Chaplain later wrote about Alastair's part in this (see below, 96). He found time to send a short letter home: "We are very comfortable here. The only thing is we are short of cigarettes, but Skeil is sending us up a lot we 'opes." Trusting that they were "all well and cheerful", he concluded his last letter to his mother, "Very much love, from your very affectionate son." He was then overtaken by preparing for the attack in which he

---

[112] Buchan, A., *Alastair Buchan*, 31-32.
[113] Ibid., 30-31; he felt selfish if they worried, *Unforgettable*, 147. *Alastair Buchan*, 30 for the next quote about his grin.

would command the Company. Later Colonel Gordon acknowledged that during the bombardment before the battle

> he had occasion to send me reports, and ask questions about equipment, etc., and various preparations in connection with the attack, and in every case I just thought to myself as I read these reports or answered the questions, "Now that is a thoroughly reliable officer, and it is a great blessing to know that he is commanding this Company."…. I shall always remember him as I saw him last about 4.45 a.m. on April 9th as I left my dug-out to go round his company for the last time. I shook hands with him and wished him good luck – a Scottish gentleman and officer.[114]

Buchan takes up the account:

> Zero hour was at 5.30 on the morning of 9th of April. At four a.m. a drizzle had begun, which changed presently to drifts of thin snow. It was bitterly cold and scarcely half light, and the troops waiting for the signal saw only a dark mist flecked with snowflakes. But at the appointed moment the British guns broke into such a fire as had not yet been seen on any battle-ground on earth. It was the first hour of the Somme repeated, but tenfold more awful. As our men went over

---

[114] Buchan, A., *Alastair Buchan*, 36-37.

the parapets they felt as if they were under the protection of some supernatural power, for the heaven above them was one canopy of shrieking steel. There were now no enemy front trenches; there were no second-line trenches – only a hummocky waste of craters and broken wire, over which our barrage crept relentlessly.

The 6/7 Scots Fusiliers were on the right and in front of the Railway Triangle, where this section "was the strongest German fortress in the neighbourhood," and "after severe fighting the triangle was carried, with the aid of tanks."[115] As Anna wrote, Alastair leading

his Company in the attack. They were in the German second line when Alastair was heavily wounded by shrapnel. At the aid-post he was so cheery that the Colonel, the Chaplain, and others wrote to us that he was only slightly wounded and he would soon be home.

Buchan followed this up with

The whole position was in our hands by 6.30 a.m. The enemy had meantime opened up a heavy barrage, and the commander of B Company, Lieutenant A. E. Buchan, fell mortally wounded.[116]

---

[115] Buchan, *Scots Fusiliers*, 376.*The Hutchesonian*, June 1917, 187: Courtesy of the Hutchesons' Educational Trust.
[116] Buchan, *Scots Fusiliers*, 376 & 377. [See endnote on p. 92]

Another account, probably from the family tells more:

> Before he fell he knew the day was won, and that
> his splendid Division had maintained their great
> record. At the aid post he was so cheery that the
> men who saw him thought that his wounds were
> slight, and wrote home that he would soon be in
> Blighty…. [but] when at five o'clock in the
> afternoon, they carried him into the Casualty
> Clearing Station nothing could be done. [Anna
> added, "his high courage had deceived them and
> his wounds were mortal."] Kind hands did what
> they could to ease him and he smiled at the doctor
> and nurse, and said he was "quite all right." He
> died in about an hour. He lies in a little graveyard
> on a bit of moorland that could be Leadburn, and
> round him lie many other "kindly Scots."[117]

Colonel Gordon later asked for more detail which was
provided by 2/Lieut. Andrew Nimmo of B Company
from eye witnesses, especially from Private W.
Wheeler:

> Mr Buchan reached the third trench having been
> wounded between the second and third trench.
> The wound was in the hip and Mr Buchan
> complained of pain in the stomach. Wheeler
> helped him from shell hole to shell hole until he
> met some R.A.M.C. men who carried Buchan to

[117] Gunn, *Book of Remembrance*, 303; Buchan, A., *Alastair Buchan*, 34.

the dressing station where he was under the care of the battalion doctor, He was buried at the clearing station.[118]

It was a time when the family were already worried about him. Buchan wrote to his mother from London on 10th April saying, "the great battle has begun and so far has gone very well." He admitted that it was an "anxious time" but "they must wait to hear if old Alastair was in it. The main brunt has been born by the Canadian Corps but I may get further information today of the troops used." He did not know that his brother was already dead when he wrote.[119]

It was the same for Helen Buchan who was always worried about her youngest son being at war. In ignorance she wrote to him on the same day, "Your dear precious letter today makes us very anxious. I see that the great push has begun and you are in it. I scarcely know what I am doing." Then she prayed that, the Everlasting Arms may be close about you in these awful days."[120] They were, but not in the way that she supposed. We will see that Walter felt the same 111).

Anna relates how further details of his death were known when Beatrice Reid, a nurse at the

---

[118] 2/Lieut Andrew Nimmo, B Company RSF, in the field, 19th April 1917, John Buchan Story Archive.
[119] Buchan to 'My Dear Wee Mother", 10th April 1917: NLS Acc.7214 Mf MSS 304.
[120] Mother to Alastair, 10th April 1917, JB Story Archive.

casualty field station, who tended Alastair's wounds, wrote to his mother. [121]

> Alastair and another boy, Gervaise Maude, were brought in together. Nothing could be done for them and they died in a few minutes. When she had washed the battle-grime from their faces and smoothed their flaxen hair, they looked mere children, and, knowing that somewhere over the Channel hearts would break for those bright heads, before they were laid in the earth she kissed them for their mothers.

From some oversight Gordon

> was not informed by the C[asualty] C[learing] station, and I had been congratulating myself that he got a comparatively slight wound and was perfectly safe. It was a terrible revulsion to hear this rumour of his death.... He was a most excellent fellow, and a thoroughly reliable and good officer."[122]

Ian Buckingham has noted how the Peebles family received "the shattering news" on "the afternoon of April 11th": "In 1917 it was the telegram boy knocking on the door with this handwritten and brief

---

[121] Buchan, A., *Unforgettable*, 150; for Beatrice Reid see Buchan, U., *Beyond*, 198. Her letter is in the JB Story Archive.
[122] Buchan, A., *Alastair Buchan*, 36.

note". The family had been right to be apprehensive about him.[123]

Regret to inform you that 2/Lt A. E. Buchan, 6th Royal Scots Fusiliers died of his wounds on April 9. The Army Council express their sympathy. Secy. War Office.

Alastair was one of "six soldiers connected with Peebles" who died on that first day of the Battle. Two more followed within days.[124] Buchan was at GHQ the following week, and went out and met his brother's fellow officers. He heard at first hand from the doctor and nurse who had tended Alastair before he died. As he had succumbed at the 41st Casualty Clearing Station Alastair's body was later re-buried in Duisans British Cemetery in Etrun, a small village north-west of Arras, which had been selected in February for casualties from the area. The first burials had only taken place the previous month. Then a sergeant took Buchan to the wooden cross on "the little grave and covered it with flowers."[125]

---

[123] Buchan, A., *Alastair Buchan*, 34: Buckingham, *Peeblesshire News*; there is a copy of the telegram to his mother in National Archives WO 339/26528.

[124] Gunn, *Book of Remembrance*, 301. Their names are recorded on memorials in the Chambers Institution Quadrangle in Peebles.

[125] Thomas, "France 1992", 13; Buchan, A., *Alastair Buchan*, 35; Buchan, U., *Beyond*, 198-199.

*25. Aerial photograph of 41 C.C.S., B.E F.
situated at Agney-le-Duisans, Pas de Calais,
France, where Alastair died of wounds on Easter
Monday, the 9th April 1917. Though clearly
marked by red crosses visible from the air, two
bomb holes are noted on the recto.*

Meanwhile, back in Peebles the family awaited the return of his effects which were forwarded on by the agents, Cox's and King's on 17th April. There is always pathos regarding a list of such items left behind, for so few are of any more than little consequence. Thus

> 1 electric torch / 1 wrist watch / 1 whistle and lanyard / 2 sleeve springs / 1 cheque book / 1 Testament / 1 Rule / 1 cigarette case (leather) / 1 Stud / 1 tobacco pouch / 1 leather photo case & photos / 1 pipe / 1 leather money case / 1 devotional book /1 identity disc / paper cutting.

"Another shattering day" was to follow. [126]

> His kit came back. All the things that he packed so gaily – we remembered everything as we took them out. It was just as he had left it – dirty clothes, etc – I washed them all myself. It is the last thing I shall do for him."

The nurse, Beatrice Reid, wrote again to Alastair's mother and in doing this she took a very strong Christian line in expressing her condolences to her and the family.

> No one could do more nobly than your son, and it must comfort you to know that he gave his life for others even as Christ did and he shall have his reward. 'Greater love hath no man than

---

[126] Anna to John, Peebles, 7th May 1917, JB Story Archive.

this....'[127]

She also used to visit the graves of Alastair and the subaltern from another regiment who died with him. We do not know whether this was unusual empathy towards those who died in her care. She certainly impressed the Buchans with her sympathetic concern and follow-up.

Endnote on Alastair's Mortal Wound (page 85ff.)

The accounts vary, and we may wonder what actually happened. The Colonel reported, and observers present like the Chaplain & others (85) make it quite clear, that Alastair bore with commendable & characteristic cheerfulness the wounds that soon proved fatal. As to their severity, Anna says that "his high courage deceived them" (86). Fusilier Wheeler's report to Gordon shows (86) that he had to be helped, with difficulty, to the battalion doctor with whom he spent the day. It is uncertain how much he knew himself. Buchan suggested that towards evening a sudden haemorrhage came on which required him to be taken to the C.C.S. (109). Nurse Reed says that when Alastair was brought in, he was brave & peaceful, barely conscious before succumbing (note 127 for her letter). Buchan also comforted himself that his brother thought that he was going home (109). Not knowing his mind or if he knew he was dying, we know the reputation he had acquired in facing danger, & how he conducted himself in the last battle.

---

[127] "that a man lay down his life for his friends." *St John's Gospel* 15:13. Reid to Mrs Buchan, 41 C.C.S., BEF, 13th September 1917 (John Buchan Story Archive). This appears to be the second letter from her, but perhaps the first to be received.

CHAPTER TEN

APPRECIATIONS

His family had come to believe that Alastair was born for the Great War, for when it "came he seemed to find himself. This was his job, this was what he had been waiting for, and he went into it with his whole heart."[128] Though he could write that "of all miserable jobs soldiering is the worst" he still added "– sometimes; but the very beastliness of it makes comfort so much more comfortable that it is well worth while", and still prefaced this with "I am very contented and happy."[129] He could say in a letter home three months before he died, "These last two years have been the happiest of my life." His letters were "uniformly cheerful."[130] His memory was constantly in the minds of his family. Despite her Christianity his mother, whom he dearly loved, blamed herself for his death and put it down to her own shortcomings in a morbid way which distressed her children. Buchan

---

[128] Buchan. A., *Alastair Buchan*, 17; Buchan, J., *Memory-Hold-the-Door*, 255.

[129] Buchan, A., *Alastair Buchan*, 26.

[130] Ibid., 18 & 29. Alastair to mother, 26th February 1917. It was a historic day, commissioned two years ago, wounded a year ago – "They have been two very happy years all things considered."

"somehow regarded him less as a brother of mine than as the eldest of the children."[131] We have seen how close Anna and Walter were to this youngest of them, his home had been so much with one or both of them, and all his siblings remarked on his extraordinarily winning nature.

There are a number of references to him as the happy warrior. This is how Stair Gillon, Buchan's Oxford friend, reacted to his death:

> When the blow came I found that it was a heavy personal blow to *me* too, for he was a splendid, attractive lad – the happy warrior if ever there was one….I suppose he was doing the very best work possible to one of his years – the capable and gallant leading of men in battle, and watching and caring for them behind the front. I could see at a glance that he was the right man in the right place, and I know what his Colonel thought of him – the very highest possible. He was just what one would like to see grow out of the little boy in the kilt that I sat next [to] at John's wedding.[132]

As was to be expected, we have seen the letter sent by his Commanding Officer, Colonel Gordon. He wrote

---

[131] Adam Smith, *John Buchan*, 205.
[132] Buchan, A., *Alastair Buchan*, 37; on 38 he goes on to compare him and his brother William to David and Jonathan. Buchan, U. *Beyond*, 199.

at the time that he regarded Alastair as "a most excellent fellow, and a thoroughly good and reliable officer." After receiving a copy of Anna's memorial book at the end of the year, he at once wrote again:

> I still think of Alastair, and shall always think of him... as I saw him at 4.45.a.m. on Easter Monday, April 9, when he looked me straight in the face and we shook hands. Of all the officers who have been killed while serving in this Battn. under me, he is one of 3 whose death I regret most deeply, but still, as Skeil says, it is something to have known such a bright happy nature.... I cannot tell you how much I appreciate Alastair's references to me, but goodness knows that I did very little for him, though I liked him very much.[133]

The Right Honourable Winston Churchill, M.P. (Alastair's Commanding Officer for the months of January and February 1916) wrote:

> He was a very charming and gallant young officer, simple, conscientious, and much liked by his comrades. I knew him well enough to understand how great his loss must be to those who knew him better, and to those who knew him best of all.[134]

---

[133] Letter from Lt-Col. E. I. D. Gordon, to Buchan, 6/7 RSF, 29th December 1917. NLS Acc.11627/37.
[134] Buchan, A., *Alastair Buchan*, 38.

From the Chaplain of the 6/7th RSF:

> He will be much missed in the battalion, in which
> he was deservedly popular. His influence among
> officers and men was all to the good. On Good
> Friday I arranged a service for his Company, and
> he did all he could to help me, and was present
> himself. My most vivid memory of that service is
> the picture of your son joining heartily in the
> hymn, 'When I survey the wondrous Cross.' He
> was standing just at my left. I suppose this was
> the last service he was at, and I thought it might
> be some comfort to you to know that I believe he
> was ready to meet his Maker for whose cause he
> was soon to give his life, 'filling up what was
> behind in the sufferings of Christ.'[135]

The Clerk of John Knox and Tradeston Church in
Glasgow (the two had merged after Mr Buchan
retired) wrote to the family. He had not been at the
church in their time and they were greatly moved by
his words:

> It was very touching to listen to the tributes from
> the old elders who had known him from his
> earliest years. He was indeed a bright spirit, and
> boundless were the hopes that those faithful
> friends centred in Alastair. It is tragic to think of
> him cut off just when life was opening up before

---

[135] Buchan, A., *Alastair Buchan*, 38-39. See below Chapter
Sixteen, 176, 182, & 186.

him with all its bright promise, but we must not measure life by years but by service, and on that standard what a full and glorious life was his!....those present were deeply affected. There is a rich and deep current of loyalty and devotion and affection towards you and all your family among the members of your old church, and we new-comers have all been drawn into it by sympathy and admiration. Words are very weak and empty at such a time as this, but they are all we have.[136]

Buchan had previously written poems in memory of his father, and his brother William, and now he wrote his own elegiac appreciation of Alastair which Anna included:

A.E.B.

Born 12th June 1894.

Died of Wounds received at Arras, 9th April 1917[137]

A mile or two from Arras town
The yellow moorland stretches far,
And from its crest the roads go down
Like arrows to the front of war.

---

[136] Buchan, A., *Alastair Buchan*, 39-40.
[137] First published in *Alastair Buchan* (1917), and then in Buchan, *Poems Scots and English* (1936 edition); reprinted by Lownie and Milne, *Collected Poems*, 152-156; Anna shortened it in *Unforgettable*, 150-152.

All day the laden convoys pass,
The sunburnt troops are swinging by,
And far above the trampled grass
The droning planes climb up the sky.

In April when I passed that way
An April joy was in the breeze:
The hollows of the woods were gay
With slender-stalked anemones.

The horn of Spring was faintly blown,
Bidding a ransomed world awake,
Nor could the throbbing batteries drown
The nesting linnets in the brake.

And as I stood beside the grave,
Where 'mid your kindly Scots you lie,
I could not think that one so brave,
So glad of heart, so kind of eye,

Had found the deep and dreamless rest,
Which men may crave who bear the scars
Of weary decades on their breast,
And yearn for slumber after wars.

You scarce had shed your boyhood's years,
In every vein the blood ran young,
Your soul uncramped by ageing fears,
Your tales untold, your songs unsung.

As if my sorrow to beguile,
I heard the ballad's bold refrain:
"I'll lay me down and bleed a-while,
And then I'll rise and fight again."

II

Long, long ago, when all the lands
Were deep in peace as summer sea,
God chose his squires, and trained their hands
For those stern lists of liberty.

You made no careful plans for life,
Happy with dreams and books and friends,
Incurious of our worldly strife,
As dedicate to nobler ends.

Like some young knight, who kept his sword
Virgin from common broils that he
Might flesh it on the Paynim horde
When Richard stormed through Galilee.

I mind how on the hills of home
You ever lagged and strayed aside,
A brooding boy whose thoughts would roam
O'er gallant fates that might betide.

But not the wildest dreams of youth,
Born of the sunset and the spring,
Could match the splendour of the truth
That waited on your journeying –

The ancient city deep in night,
The wind among its crumbling spires;
The assembly in the chill twilight
Murky with ghosts of wayward fires;

The last brave words; the outward march;
The punctual shells, whose ceaseless beat
Made the dark sky an echoing arch
Pounded without by demon feet.

While with the morn wild April blew
Her snows across the tortured mead,
The spring-time gales that once you knew
In glens beside the founts of Tweed.

And then the appointed hour; the dread
Gun-flare that turned the sleet to flame,
When, the long vigil o'er, you led
Your men to purge the world of shame.

I know that in your soul was then
No fear to irk or hate to mar,
But a strong peace and joy as when
The Sons of God go forth to war.

You did not fail till you had won
The utmost trench and knew the pride
Of a high duty nobly done
And a great longing satisfied.

You left the line with jest and smile
And heart that would not bow to pain –
"I'll lay me down and bleed a-while,
And then I'll rise and fight again."

III

We cannot grieve that youth so strong
Should miss the encroaching frosts of age,
The sordid fears, the unnerving throng
Of cares that are man's heritage.

A boy in years, you travelled far
And found perfection in short space;
By the stern sacrament of war
You grew in gifts and power and grace,

Until, with soul attuned and tried,
You reached full manhood, staunch and free,
And bore a spirit o'er the tide
Most ripe for immortality.

We cannot tell what grave pure light
Illumes for you our earthly show,
What heavenly love and infinite
Wisdom is yours; but this we know -

That just beyond our senses veil
You dwell unseen in youth and joy,
Joy which no languid years can pale
Youth which is younger than the boy.

Your kindly voice enhearten still,
Your happy laughter is not dead,
And when we roam our Border hill
You walk beside with lighter tread.

All day where lies your valiant dust
The troops go by to hold the line;
They never steel for ward or thrust
But you are with them, brother mine.

Still, still you list the ancient tunes,
The comrade fire is with you yet;
Still, still you lead your worn platoons
Beyond the farthest parapet.

And when to chaos and black night
At last the broken eagles flee,
Your heart will know the stern delight
Of his who succours liberty.

*   *   *   *   *   *

I stood beside your new-made grave,
And as I mused my sorrow fled,
Save for those mortal thoughts that crave
For sight of those who men call dead.

I knew you moved in ampler powers,
A warrior in a purer strife,
Walking that world that shall be ours
When death has called us dead to life.

The rough white cross above your breast,
The earth ungraced by flower or stone,
Are bivouac marks of those who rest
One instant ere they hasten on.

More fit such grave than funeral pile,
Than requiem dirge and ballad strain:
"I'll lay me down and bleed a-while,
And then I'll rise and fight again."

Alan Riach, of the University of Glasgow, has recently called it "a noble lament." Here is Anna's reaction:

> I must tell you how much we loved your poem. It is so beautiful and simple and true. It seems to me about the best thing you have ever done. That ballad refrain ['I'll lay me down....'] was an inspiration and the whole thing is just like the dear gentle laddie. It is an infinite comfort to us.[138]

Nearly her last memory of Alastair was of playing a mock battle with their nephew, Mr John, and how gentle he was with little children.

After the War, in 1919 or 1920, the Peebles family will have received the Next of Kin Memorial Plaque in bronze, and the parchment Scroll with the King's Message. They will also have received the medals awarded to Alastair: the 1914-15 Star, the

---

[138] Riach, Professor of Scottish Literature, in *The National*, 5th November 2018. Anna to Buchan, Peebles, 23rd June 1917.

British War Medal, and the Victory Medal.[139] His name is included on a number of War Memorials including those found at Peebles, Hutchesons', Glasgow University, and at the Scottish National in Edinburgh Castle.

In 1925, the Prince of Wales, as Colonel-in-Chief of the Royal Scots Fusiliers, wrote a Preface to Buchan's *History* of the Regiment. The author did not include a dedication, but it was provided by the Prince in a double compliment:

> The whole work of compiling and publishing this book has been undertaken by John Buchan (who has old family connections with the regiment) as a memorial to his brother, who fought and died gallantly in the Great War serving with the Royal Scots Fusiliers.

Buchan was generous in acknowledging the help of others in compiling the work.[140] Then in his 1936 edition of *Poems Scots and English*, Buchan included the lines to "A.E.B." already fully quoted, and presumably written just too late for inclusion in the first edition in 1917. He kept Alastair's memory before the public.

---

[139] I presume that he qualified for all three. I know from my father's experience that if you were on the Western Front for at least one month before the end of 1915 (Alastair just), you would receive the "1914-1914 Star" later.

[140] Buchan and Stewart, *Scots Fusiliers*, v & vii-viii.

Buchan did so in more veiled ways. We have seen his poem in Lallans, on page xxii, celebrating the Royal Scots Fusiliers and their courage. The fictional character in *Mr Standfast*, Geordie Hamilton has also been mentioned, celebrating one of the corporals who "looked out" for Alastair in the trenches. He is described in *Mr Standfast* as "one of the adorable bandy-legged stocky type that went through the Railway Triangle at Arras as though through blotting paper."[141] In that action Alastair was mortally wounded. In the same book there is "Captain Robert Blaikie of the Scots Fusiliers." [142] This is the alias Hannay adopts in a tight corner. He then meets young Broadbury, a wounded subaltern of whom he reflects: "It is the type that makes dashing regimental officers, and earns V.C.s, and gets done in wholesale." It is clear who he had in mind (see below, 128-129).

Buchan knew about trench warfare from various sources, though Alastair's experience was almost wholly limited to it. Paul Webb wrote that Buchan "makes trench warfare interesting and exciting; it is fascinating to have the Western Front

---

[141] The quotations are in Buchan, J., *Mr Standfast*, FOUR/65, and FIVE/85 in the Polygon edition. In real life, Hamilton was later commissioned.

[142] Blaikie may be a reminiscence of that Captain Ritchie who, with his wife, was "exceedingly kind" to Alastair at Queensferry. Later, he was with the 6/7 battalion on the day that her brother was mortally wounded, and Anna wrote then that "It is good to think of him being with a band of brothers. There is no loneliness in such a death." Anna to Buchan, Peebles, 13th April 1917, JB Story Archive.

presented in a totally different light to that brought to bear on our sensibilities by the war poets like Sassoon and Owen."[143]

Again, in *The Dancing Floor* a character is used to reflect Alastair. He and the fictional Vernon Milburne come of evangelical families and stick to these beliefs in life. Both were "self-absorbed" boys rather disinterested in the future, and to his family Alastair's end was predestined too, born for the war. Leithen's only nephew Charles, newly gazetted as a wartime officer, also pleads to be sent overseas. After being drilled by a Guards sergeant, the description of Alastair in Leithen serving in France is pretty exact:

> it was a long dismal grind, but I had the inestimable advantage of good health, and I was never a day off duty because of sickness. I suppose I enjoyed it in a sense; anyhow I got tremendously keen about my new profession, and rose in it far quicker than I deserved. [See 79, 80]

Almost the last thing Buchan did was to ask Anna to find the photographs for *Memory-Hold-the-Door*. Limited to ten, only three were of family, his wife, eldest son, and Alastair, who was preferred to his parents, his sister Anna, his brother Walter and more surprisingly to William, called his *Fratri Dilectissimo* in the memorial poem of 1912. Apart from Walter, Anna added these in her memoirs.

---

[143] Webb, *Buchan Companion*, 79.

CHAPTER ELEVEN

POST MORTEM

In November 1917, Anna published her novel *The Setons*, "an attempt to reconstruct for her [mother] our home-life in Glasgow." Her father was in it and Alastair (called Buff), "all his funny ways and sayings as far as I could remember them." She dedicated it to her mother, in memory of William and Alastair:

> *They sought the glory of their country,*
> *They see the glory of God.*

(She also represented him elsewhere in her fiction and could make the reader feel that he was someone they had always known.)[144]

Before the end of the year this was followed by her memorial volume, *Alastair Buchan 1894-1917*. It contains clear statements that Alastair died a believing Christian. However, such was the commitment of the family, that the consolation of being risen with Christ was assumed and not overtly stated at the time. Perhaps it was unnecessary in a reticent age to emphasise what they could all take as read. The sister of their ordained friend Robbie Macmillan, who was

---

[144] Buchan, A., *Unforgettable*, 155-156; Thomas, "France 1992", 14.

26. Anna's volume

killed two days later, is equally restrained about both
in exchanging supportive letters with the Buchans.
Then some of Buchan's immediate correspondence
sheds an interesting light on how they expressed the
way they coped with this bereavement, and how we
should interpret it. Here is perhaps the first letter to his
surviving brother, Walter, after receiving the news by
telegram. "Nan" is Anna.

76 Portland Place, W.
April 14 '17

My dearest old Walter,
I enclose a letter from Alastair's Colonel. It is a
mercy we got the wire first. He writes of course
from the battlefield. Alastair's wound was not

thought serious and he was moved to a field hospital. Probably some haemorrhage came on in the evening and he died. He had the satisfaction of knowing that we were winning and that he had done most awfully well, and he was probably very happy thinking he was on the way home. When the officer [Gordon] says that he was a 'thoroughly reliable officer' I know that is the highest praise he could give. I know how sad he will be over Alastair's death.

How am I to comfort you my poor old man? I know all the laddie meant to you and to Nan. It is the bitterest cup that could have been placed before you. But you and Nan are very brave, and you will bear up for the sake of the brave fellow who is gone. We shall get further details I hope on Thursday. And if Alastair had to die I think the circumstances are all I should have wanted. He must have got the satisfaction of victory and he can't have suffered much or long.

Tommy Nelson [the publisher, and Buchan's partner] was killed instantaneously by a shell.

Mother is a splendid wee body. I hope her eye will be all right. The one thing we must all do now is to cultivate courage and to strive to make Alastair's sacrifice and that of all the others not in vain for the world.

I send you this letter, [lost] which is from a Canadian officer I never heard of. He must have read of it in the paper.

You and I and Nan are all that is left of a family now. We must be everything to each other.

Yours affectionately,

John

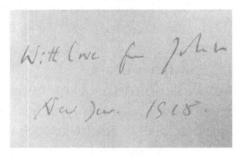

27. Buchan's dedication in a copy of the memorial volume Alastair Buchan 1894-1917.

In his reply to Buchan's letter, [145] Walter echoed Buchan's fortitude.

Your letters are a great comfort. We must all try to bear up, but just now it is difficult. I feel as if

---

[145] See NLS. Acc.11627/37. The pressure of Buchan's other responsibilities and his grief are evident in the letter in the uncharacteristic repetition of the words 'officer' and 'brave' as well as the even worse than usual scribbled illegibility of his hand. I am grateful for Ursula Buchan's ready help over four seemingly undecipherable places. In the collected Buchan Letters on microfilm (NLS) there is a gap between 10th April - May 1917, as though those items were too personal to be included there.

a great part of my life had suddenly been taken away and I don't seem to be much interested in what is left. I did not realise how much the Mhor's companionship meant to me. I tried to do my best for him and to see him through the rough places. I was looking forward to help in his future. What futile hopes. His future was safe but not in this world. He was willing to lay down his perfect youth, and his last wish for those left behind was that they should be cheerful. We must try to obey that wish but it is hard. Who shall dare to sorrow for our splendid young brother? I envy him the manner of his going and a great part of my heart lies with him now.[146]

What of the two ladies, Helen and Anna? The grieving in Peebles was great. People kept coming to the house to say how sorry they were. Anna, soon after they heard the news wrote that

His last message was cheerfulness and whenever I can stop crying I mean to keep a cheery face. We must remember 'Toujours, smiley face' [as he had written of himself].

She added, "Poor Mother is wonderfully brave and good but oh! My dear we have very sore hearts." Helen did not feel like writing letters for weeks and

---

[146] Walter to Buchan, Peebles, 16th April 1917, JB Story Archive.

later took "very long walks. She says the putting one foot before another is a sort of relief."

Anna immediately consoled herself in a number of ways. As she wrote later more than once, she found comfort in that they had been able to give him such a happy time as he grew up. There was nothing he ever wanted that they did not try to give him.

She rejoiced that Susie's children, Alice and Mr John would have treasured memories of an uncle who would never grow old.

Their Christian faith came through when Anna agreed with Alastair that even the sad times had been worth it, explaining that they "made him sit lightly to the things of the world." Perhaps he thought so little about his future because he felt it "wasn't to be spent here." He had told them, "Remember, I shan't mind going."

> And to Alastair who loved drama [as she did] what a stage setting for the last act! Sometimes I used to laugh to myself at the little delicate timid boy who told himself such stories of stirring deeds with himself as hero. But in our wildest dreams we could never have imagined a more glorious death under more awe-inspiring circumstances. The ruins and town of Arras, the wild April weather, the thunder, the guns, and the last wild rush.

Perhaps most of all there were the vivid memories of his unfailing cheerfulness. [147]

It must be said that because they all believed the Christian hope, they did not need to repeat it to each other. Beyond that, when "Steve" was killed Alastair had quoted from Baring's lines on Julian Grenfell in writing to his friend's father to describe how he felt:

Because of you we will be glad and gay,
[Remembering you, we will be brave and strong]; [148]

That couplet was the apt expression, not the source, of how the family endeavoured to cope. In grieving for Alastair, Buchan encouraged Walter by writing this: "But you and Nan are very brave, and you will bear up for the sake of the brave fellow who is gone." This expresses Buchan's desire for fortitude.[149] Even earlier still Anna tells us that the family reaction to William's death before the war had been just the same, predating Baring – "And seeing him so brave for very shame's

---

[147] In these two paras., all about Helen, and by and about Anna, is found in these letters, Anna to Susie, Peebles, 13th April, in Anna to John, Peebles, 7th May, & in Anna to Susie, Broughton Green, 22nd August 1917.

[148] Baring, "To Julian Grenfell".

[149] Greig, "In Journeyings….", 17, pointed out that Buchan had to show fortitude in the challenges he faced in "contending against odds": also in supporting himself, in adapting to new environments, in coping with chronic illness and, we might add, facing bereavement over the death of family and friends. This had a Christian basis, below 132-133, 187-188 & 194-195.

sake we were brave too."[150] Such sentiments echoed the Buchan siblings' attitude in bereavement. In all senses the two young Buchan men died well.[151] In addition to their Christian faith the family would seek to adopt the stiff upper lip in bereavement, and in doing that they were well prepared.

They remembered Alastair always. We have seen that Anna did this much more explicitly. At the end of her memorial volume, she wrote:

> For two and twenty years we kept him – not a long span of years; but we can smile through our tears when we think of the rounded, perfect, complete life that was his. Twenty-two years of straightness and gentleness and mirth, and then the end. And such an end!

Then, summing up Alastair's life, she quoted:

> The message came to him as it came to the pilgrim. "...He expects thee at His table to sup with Him in His Kingdom the next day after Easter."[152]

This was probably at the suggestion of Buchan, finding consolation in his familiar Bunyan.

Walter was at once determined that there should be a proper portrait of Alastair.

---

[150] Buchan, A., *Unforgettable*, 136.
[151] Gillon in *Alastair Buchan*, 38; Buchan, J., *Memory*, 356.
[152] Buchan, A., *Alastair Buchan*, 41.

I enclose a postcard of Alastair. I am very anxious that a good picture should be painted from it, if at all possible. It is so like him. Will you see what can be done… and by a first class artist. I don't care what it costs, for it should be handed down as a very precious possession. I will send other photographs, but I like that one best.[153]

In response, Buchan promised to see William Orpen in France as soon as possible, but knew that he disliked painting from a photograph.[154] Nevertheless, he agreed to do that, and no charge was made for the result in oils which was not delivered until ten years later.

In 1919 Anna did her own thing. By donating £105, the Buchan Prize for Poetry (or for the best poem on a given subject) was to be awarded annually at the University of Glasgow by the Professors of English Literature and Scottish History and Literature. The income would be five pounds.[155] They were the

---

[153] Walter to Buchan, Peebles, 16th April 1917, JB Story Archive.

[154] Buchan responded to Walter's suggestion and within two days discussed the commission with Orpen in France: Buchan to Walter, Portland Place, 18th April 1917, NLS Acc.11627/37; for no fee, Buchan, U., *Beyond*, 199. Orpen was employed by the War Office as a war artist.

[155] NLS Acc.11627/37: Letter of thanks for the cheque to Anna from the Principal, Sir Donald MacAllister, 6th December 1919. It was known as "The Alastair Buchan Prize"; in 2017 the awards were First, £200, Second, £100, Third £50.

two closest siblings to Alastair and knew him best. Buchan may have paid for it indirectly, but Anna certainly sent it in and, given her inheriting everything of William's, [156] it was more than natural that she who knew Alastair best of all should do so.

All of these incidents reflect the way the Buchans coped with Alastair's death. Not unnaturally there was a certain amount of lionising in the way they remembered him. It was notorious that young subalterns often survived in the trenches for only a few weeks. When Alastair's two spells of such service are calculated they amount to no more than that. Probably all the Peebles family, and certainly Buchan and Anna, had prepared themselves by believing that Alastair would not survive the war.

It in no way dishonours his memory to say that his death was not dramatically heroic. He received his mortal wound while faithfully carrying out his military duties. At the time nothing more could have been asked of him. He was never placed in a situation where exceptional valour was required. It was certainly tragic that such an engaging young man gave his life before ever reaching his prime, or being able to use his gifts to the full. He was a promising young officer, but as yet largely untried in action.

Henry Fairlie, as a youth between the Wars, was uncomfortable with the idyll of youth and promise

---

[156] British Library, Asian and African Collection, IOR/L/AG/34/29/158 pages 39-40 and 104-105.

which Buchan, and others, adopted as their way of remembering 'doomed youth' – that immortal part 'which knows not age or weariness or defeat.' He felt that

> these lives had not been tested; they were tested in their deaths; and each of them passed, one almost expects to read *summa cum laude* [with great distinction]. For, some of us who were reared with the idyll sung in our ears, it became increasingly objectionable. It seemed as if the survivors felt no anger at the slaughter of their friends, as if their sorrow at these vanished lives was sweet to them. They did not seem to remember how their friends died...

and instead they recalled them as eternally young.[157]

He would have found the family guilty on all points, and something of that reaction in Buchan's poem of appreciation, and Anna's memorial volume, as well as Walter's urgent desire for a portrait, had he known of them. Their baby brother had grown up to become their hero, and why not? There was nothing in his life or death to mar their affectionate memory of him. On the contrary, though they were proud of him, there is no doubt that they always deeply mourned his loss, and it nearly killed their mother. They had one consolation denied to many others, a grave to visit (see

---

[157] Fairlie, *The Kennedy Promise*, 117-118.

below, 123). He seemed not to have suffered greatly and to have died peacefully.

Fairlie may not have appreciated that to this Christian family Alastair's death was not a despairing disappearance into nothingness. To his siblings he had preceded them, like Violet, William and their Father into that eternity which knows not "sorrow or death or crying or pain," pioneered by Jesus in his resurrection and subsequent ascension into heaven.[158] Because of their belief it was not insensitive to celebrate him now released from the bonds of mortality, as well as for a time to mourn for him as "one who men call dead" until they joined him, with the others of their family and friends who had gone before them in their Christian pilgrimage. Though Fairlie's criticism is understandable, it is overblown. Of course they remembered them as eternally young, because that was the only way they had known them.

Besides, it was not just the family that tended to idolise Alastair. Two days after the news was received Bank House was the scene of "people all coming continually with notes and cards to tell us how sorry they are." The minister, Donald Maclean, told Helen and Anna that

> he never addressed such a sad meeting as that in Peebles last night. Everybody is so sad about the

---

[158] *The Revelation of St John the Divine*, 21:4. They believed Jesus would "take them to Himself." *St John's Gospel*, 14:3.

fair-haired laddie that trudged about so gaily. They have been so good and taken such an interest in him.

Sometimes they just wished that they could be alone.[159]

Even more strikingly, perhaps there were the tributes from his contemporary brother officers. Some of the most moving were from men of his own rank or below him. "Old Skeil", once a fellow subaltern and now his Company Commander wrote of Anna's memoir [160] that

the whole book reveals his straight forward and buoyant spirit. Personally I value his references to me more highly than anything else that has come my way in life. It was like him to mention my name in the cheery generous hearted way he did, and I take infinite comfort in the thought that I was helpful to him and that he thought of me kindly. More than ever now do I realise how his very presence gave a brighter aspect to things, and drove away some of that seriousness that is apt to be ever present out here. I had to meet his light-heartedness half way and both of us benefitted.

[159] Anna to Susie, Peebles, 13th April 1917. JB Story Archive.
[160] Skeil to Buchan, 6/7 RSF, B Coy, 30th December 1917: NLS Acc. 11627/37.

A fellow subaltern (later killed) wrote: "He kept us all up, for he was the only one whose spirits never went down. He was the Happy Warrior, if ever there was one. I don't like to say he was my great friend, but he was my hero, and I hung on his words."[161]

From another brother officer:

> Dear brave old Alastair has gone to join the Grenfells and the Brookes and the other splendid heroes. How hard it must be for you to part with him. But what beautiful memories he leaves behind him! If only we could see through our tears, we would see the triumphal march of his great young soul through the Valley of the Shadow to the Celestial Country.... What would I not give to leave such a fragrant garland of memories behind me when my time comes, as he did.[162]

It is worth recording, too, that "Arras '17" is one of the battle honours on the regimental colours of the RSF. Alastair died at the beginning of a major battle, not in some random incident like the brave, battle-hardened Smith. He was physically confronting Germans inside their territory, not separated by a hundred yards of No-Man's-Land. He had what it took in face to face conflict, and in command of a greater number of men than was usual for one of his rank.

---

[161] Gunn, *Book of Remembrance*, 303.
[162] Ibid., 304.

The family were right. Tributes like these took a lot of guts to deserve, and there is courage in how you cope with the endless threat and presence of maiming and death. To merit this last comparison from a brother officer is extraordinary. Julian Grenfell, and his cousins Francis and Riversdale, were following noted family soldiers and died heroically early in the War. One of the twins had already won the Victoria Cross, and Buchan would write a book about them.[163] Rupert Brooke died of disease on his way to his first action, but was such a celebrated poet of doomed youth. Max Hastings wrote of Julian that he was "idolised by his peers for reasons mystifying to posterity."[164] One can see why, but not everyone will agree with his assessment.

A private soldier stood by the wooden cross on Alastair's grave on Christmas morning 1917 near where he might soon lie himself, and sent these verses to Mrs Helen Buchan showing his knowledge of the personal background as well as his respect for this officer which also allowed for his familiarity:

> *Laddie that sought the glory*
> *Of God, and your country too,*
> *I bend at your grave – not in pity:*
> *In sorrow – but not for you.*

---

[163] Buchan, J., *Francis and Riversdale Grenfell.*
[164] Hastings, *Catastrophe: 1914*, 527-528.

The hills of the South are misty,
The Tweed sings a song of lament,
While your folk walk quiet and broken,
And a mother sits weeping and bent.

Yet they ask not that they should recover
The gift that to Honour they gave –
That you should ride back from the venture
Leading your gallant brave.

Content they to live in the largesse
Bequeathed of your dreamful mind,
That left no will but goodwill,
And that to all mankind.

Dear boy, when this long night is over
And Liberty's walls are rebuilt,
Surely April flowers will be fairer
In the fields where your blood was spilt:

And children shall play 'neath the green trees,
Rich valleys with gold will dance,
Because you gave to Freedom
Your soul – and your dust to France.[165]

---

[165] For the poem, see Gunn, *Book of Remembrance*, 306-307. Regarding his "goodwill…to all mankind", Anna wrote, "he could never manage even to dislike the Germans", *Alastair Buchan,* 16, cf. above 31, note 41. Buchan picked up the same point in his poem already quoted – "I know that in your soul was then / no fear to irk or hate to mar" (see above 100).

Unlike so many others, the Buchans did not live to be haunted by imagining the agonised and often lingering way their loved one died. He was not brought home terribly maimed, and there was the remembrance of a couple of happy times when his brother had seen him at the Front. They could believe that his passing had been stoical, short and comparatively peaceful. They will have known that, when combined, these were unusual privileges granted to few, and they could be consoled by them.

Moreover, all the family were blessed in having a grave to visit. Buchan had done this almost at once. In 1919, Helen Buchan, with Anna and Walter, went to Duisans. In the same year the family arranged for a replica of the wooden cross to be erected with the other lairs in the family plot in St Andrews Cemetery just outside Peebles (see Illustration 29).[166] At first the surrounding area in France was still in desolation, but those graves were in "a peaceful upland place, with larks singing overhead and daffodils blowing in the grass."

In later years the crosses were replaced by the headstones, and the countryside recovered. Helen, and

---

[166] The replica was restored in 2017, 143. The very first cross marking his grave will not have been as elaborate as the one shown in 126, Illus.29, but very simple, and made of just two pieces of wood (see endnote on p.127). The more detailed, white painted one may have been in place by the time the family first visited in 1919.

28. Duisans: Anna (hand on Alastair's Gravestone), with their mother

some of the family, continued to visit every April.[167] This was combined with the Peebles family making their annual visit to Elsfield and then to St Columba's Church, in London. [168] Alastair will have been much in mind as they received the sacrament of Holy Communion there from Buchan's hands in a building with such strong Scottish military connections.

Anna records how her mother died in 1937: [169]

On her last day on earth she woke from a short sleep with a look on her face of utter content,

---

[167] Buchan, A., *Unforgettable*, 173-175; Thomas, "France 1992", 12-14.

[168] Buchan, A., ibid., 173-175; *St Columba's Magazine*, 44-46.

[169] Buchan, A., *Unforgettable*, 211.

the look we had seen long years before when she held the youngest of us in her arms. When I leant over her, she said, "It was Alastair, he came and lay down beside me," and we wondered if she were being given back all she had lost.

At Easter 2017 the present Buchan members gathered round the family memorial in Peebles cemetery. They had restored in replica the painted wooden cross that marked Alastair's resting place near Arras, prior to the present stone. Thus on the one hundredth anniversary of his death it was rededicated by the Very Reverend Professor Ian Bradley, a member of the John Buchan Society, and that event was recorded in my letter published two days later on the 11th April 2017.

To the Editor of *The Times*

Sir,

Magnus Linklater's moving account of Scots at the battle of Arras (10 April) mentions a comment by John Buchan. His 22 year old brother, Alastair, was a Lieutenant in the Royal Scots Fusiliers, who had previously been wounded and invalided back to Scotland. The family memoir recounts that with curious prescience, Alastair loved *Cyrano de Bergerac* as a child, especially "behind the walls at Arras." Standing on the back of the sofa he would ask, "Who are these men who rush on death?" and

*29. The Family Rededication at Peebles on Sunday,
9th April 2017: Professor Ian Bradley and
the Honourable Edward Buchan*

then with a wave of his sword he would jump off, shouting "Cadets of Gascony are we…." He died of wounds received on the first day at Arras. The family held its own rededication at Peebles on Sunday.

Later that year The Great War Project at Glasgow (see below) hosted an evening of music and poetry in the Memorial Chapel of the university on the 15th November. They did this to honour Alastair, commemorating a hundred years after his death. It was entitled "This World that We Seem to Inherit":

Readings and Music for Remembrance. His great niece, Lady Stewartby, was one of the readers.

Endnote: The Great War Project at Glasgow

The information here comes from Euan Loarridge, Blog Editor for the Project. The quotation is taken from the end of *Sunset Song* by Lewis Grassic Gibbon: "So lest we shame them, let us believe that the new oppressions and foolish greeds are no more than mists that pass. They died for a world that is past, but they did not die for this that we seem to inherit." The quotation continues, "Beyond it and us there shines a greater hope and a newer world undreamt." Gibbon wrote this as the conclusion to a sermon by the local minister.

Endnote: The Original Wooden Cross

Successively, there were probably three of these. The first, simply two pieces of wood fixed together, was that visited by Buchan (see above, 89, presumably at the Casualty Clearing Station). After the body had been reinterred at Duisans, a proper memorial was installed on the 3rd May 1917. It was "made of oak, stained to a darkish hue and the lettering is cut deep and painted black."

The installation was overseen by Henry Chicheley Haldane (1872-1957), an Edinburgh solicitor and friend of Buchan who wrote to him about the details.[170] Too old to be a combatant he served on the Staff and was mentioned-in-despatches five times, O.B.E. In this letter, written on the day, he added a sketch and then commented about the inscription that "I think this is nicer than putting [it] on the cross itself. The inscription reads:

---

[170] Haldane to Buchan, HQ VI Corps BEF, 3rd May 1917), JB Story Archive; *Who Was Who*.

Lt A. E. Buchan
6/7 Royal Scots Fusiliers.
Killed in action
9th April 1917"

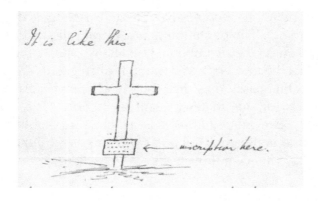

Presumably this was later replaced by a more elaborate one painted white, redundant when the CWGC headstone was put up. Taken back to Peebles, it was re-erected among the family lairs, and renewed in replica there in 2017 (above, 125-126).

Endnote: Fictional References to Alastair

Some say that Buchan represented himself best in the lawyer, Edward Leithen, but his widow pointed out that reminiscences do not amount to autobiography (*Wife and Friends*, 287). Even so, Alastair is noticeably reflected in the early pages of *The Dancing Floor* (above, 106). Earlier, still raw from losing his brother, Buchan had written *Mr Standfast* between July 1917 and July 1918 (Strachan, 'Introduction', vi.) In scattered allusions, rather than in a single character, it is this novel which most memorialises Alastair.

Hannay's batman, Corporal Geordie Hamilton of the RSF has already been encountered, as has Blaikie, based on Captain Ritchie (above, 105, note142). The very mention of such names recalls Alastair's affection for real people. The Regiment is often mentioned, and on rejoining his brigade Hannay found that his Scots Fusilier battalion had lost so many men that it had to be merged with the remnants of one from another division, as well as "bringing about a dozen officers from the training unit at home." (Ch.12/170) Alastair had been one such in this clear description of the merging of the 6th and 7th RSF under Colonel Gordon. Like Alastair, Hannay did not hate "the ordinary Boche" in the trenches. (Ch.14/199) At Arras the young subaltern Broadbury received "a bit of shrapnel in his thigh, which had played the deuce with the sciatic nerve, and he was still on crutches." (Ch.5/85) This may give further details about Alastair's similar wound received while serving at "Plugstreet". As the Colonel was proud of his son, so was Buchan of Alastair. Then Hannay was no coward, but said that it is usual to be afraid of what can torture and destroy. "The natural thing is always to be a little scared, like me, but by an effort of the will and attention to work to contrive to forget it." (Ch.21/313) This contrasts with the pacific Wake, who "never gave it a thought." Hannay sounds like Alastair who called himself "the weaker sex" (above, 53) in comparison with Hamilton and Dobson who are more like Wake.

Finally, in describing Wake's death, Buchan used detail from Alastair. Of course, circumstances are entirely different, but the cause is similar. Both men were vigorously involved in battle, & exposed to fierce enemy fire. They survive for a while unscathed & were then mortally wounded in the groin by a random piece of shrapnel. With some difficulty they are helped to comparative safety & medical help, "walking at first with support and then carried on a stretcher." Both linger for a while barely conscious "bleeding internally and no surgeon on earth could have saved [them]." Both died on the same day they were hit. (Ch. 21/324 – quotations from *Mr Standfast* are in the Polygon edition)

Though dedicated to the South African Brigade, this whole book is a remembrance of Alastair and the heroic triumph of his cause, for he had not died in vain. Moreover, *The Pilgrim's Progress* captivated both the Buchans and Peter Pineaar. Buchan's son, William, wrote that "the structure of the book reflects the Pilgrim's route and the chapters named from Bunyan's work are key to the development of Buchan's mystery." (Quoted in Macdonald, *Companion*, 127) She comments that "someone who could have fought in the war, but did not, is suspect; someone who had fought and died, in the war, was for ever heroic." This is how the Buchans remembered Alastair, with characteristic links with Mr Standfast, Mr Valiant-for-Truth, and Christian winning his way to the Celestial city where "He awaits thee at His table the next day after Easter.". ..." (see above, 114)

Here, and on pages 105-106, fifteen examples have been quoted of allusions to Alastair throughout *Mr Standfast* and elsewhere. Doubtless, some of these references were deliberate, others may have been included more subconsciously. Buchan began the book in July 1917, barely three months after Alastair's death. References, conscious or not, are no surprise when the tragedy which had overwhelmed this beloved younger brother was so fresh in the eldest sibling's mind, and of all the family. We can leave the women with Anna nursing her happy pride amid the tears, and his mother finding consolation in the regular steps she took on her very long walks. Of the two remaining brothers, there is Walter longing for the heirloom of a portrait by a good artist regardless of the cost, (above 114-115) and there is Buchan at his writing.

CHAPTER TWELVE

WHAT IF ALASTAIR HAD LIVED?

Like so many young subalterns from all over the Empire, Alastair showed himself to have been courageous, though probably above average in competence and well able to convey his cheerful encouragement to all ranks. We have seen that his family, quite naturally, mourned him grievously and saw his death as heroic. This is especially apparent in Buchan's letters and poem, and Anna's writing about him.

However, without detracting from this, and seeming dismissive, it must be pointed out that Alastair's battle experience was negligible. He took part in no major action, except briefly on his last morning, and almost all his trench warfare was engaged in holding the line opposing an equally static enemy. Sporadically, they would "stir one another up" with salvoes of artillery, and occasional small arms fire. They were not employed in leaping into enemy positions and often engaging in hand to hand fighting. He probably only went over the top in assault once, on the day he died, though sometimes having gone into No Man's Land on night patrol in activities such as repairing wire or removing that of the enemy. Routine service in the trenches was often dull, dirty, but dangerous too. The battalion War Diary shows that even on a "Quiet Day" an officer or man might be killed by enemy action or accident. Even in rest they were likely to be in range of enemy artillery and gas. His dying action was against a heavily shelled enemy, and though successful, he was not mortally wounded in personal confrontation but by shrapnel resulting from random artillery retaliation. Nevertheless, it is impressive that he had gained a reputation for bravery among his fellows, though he had no opportunity to achieve distinction. There is no doubt that he must be remembered as a gallant young man.

All of this comment is only really important if we engage in idle speculation about his future. Alastair loved people, and his eldest brother wrote this about him;

> He had a remarkable gift for managing men, especially bad characters, and he endeared himself to all who served with him. He was never out of temper or depressed, and wherever he was he diffused an air of confidence and hope.... during the last stages of the battle of the Somme I thought him the only cheerful thing in a grey world. He managed to get the best out of everybody, and won a general affection because he himself gave out so much of it. I wonder if the future historian will realise how much of the strength of the British army was due to the boys of twenty who brought the kindly ardour of youth

into the business of war and died before they could lose their freshness.[171]

Though that was written by his admiring sibling, it only summarises what we have seen others thought about him. Moreover, at both Sutton Veny and Queensferry he was kept behind for months from active service in order to train men, evidently because of "his remarkable gift for managing" them.

We have seen that some have described Alastair as the "happy warrior – if ever there was one" (94, 120). This means something very different from being gung-ho about the horrors of war, for which Julian Grenfell has been criticised, and the opposite of enjoying war for its own sake. Both Alastair and Skeil seem to have been possessed of the kind of qualities which Wordsworth expressed in his poem "The Character of the Happy Warrior." Many of his lines appear to apply to them. The poem is worth quoting in full, but here two extracts must be sufficient illustration.

> *But he, if he be called upon to face*
> *Some awful moment to which Heaven has*
> *joined*
> *Great issues, good or bad for human kind,*
> *Is happy as a Lover; and attired*

---

[171] Buchan, J., *Memory-Hold-the-Door*, 255; cf. contrary note by Crawford, 49 note 66. J. H. Beith ("Ian Hay") shared Buchan's view .

With sudden brightness, like a Man inspired....
Or if an unexpected call succeed,
Come when it will, is equal to the need:
He who, though thus endued as with a sense
And faculty for storm and turbulence,
Is yet a soul whose master-bias leans
To homefelt pleasures and to gentle scenes;
Sweet images! Which, wheresoe'er he be,
Are at his heart; and such fidelity
It is his darling passion to approve;
More brave for this, that he hath much to
    love;...

Alastair and Skeil are said to have "hated the whole thing" and yet were able to remain positive and cheerful in facing the horrors and the threats, but still happiest when at home. Then again:

And while the mortal mist is gathering, draws
His breath in confidence of Heaven's applause:

Though others may have found different ways of doing so, and many will not, these seem to have been men whose sincerity of Christian belief enabled them to overcome any natural feelings of hostility towards an enemy who had killed close friends and daily threatened them. Such lines will have been in the minds of others as well as the Buchan family who, under their father, quoted much poetry around the table, including Wordsworth. With Alastair, I think these characteristics were innate traits rather than him aspiring consciously to imitate a model such as Wordsworth had found in Nelson.

Had Alastair survived, he had wonderful qualities for a regular officer. Shortly before he died he wrote home that he had never been happier in his life than in the last two years.[172] His early ambition to be a soldier had been fulfilled, and one can imagine

31. The Rededication:
Lord Tweedsmuir and heir

him wanting to continue in that profession after the end of the war, having now found a clear path ahead.

Commanding officers who had to write to the relatives of those killed while serving under them

---

[172] Buchan, A., *Alastair Buchan*, 18.

necessarily emphasised the best, but it would appear that Alastair was particularly well thought of in the regiment, and especially by Gordon who already had battle experience, and "who survived the war after leading… in a dozen major actions."[173] Alastair would have served with him in some of these, and by the time of the Armistice he might well have been decorated. One can imagine Skeil having pressed hard to get Alastair, by then a young Captain, released from other duties to assist as a Company Commander in Russia.

Thereafter, he could have continued to serve, enjoying the company of his men, and doing his best for them, as he rose in seniority and served in various theatres between the wars. He would have been a good regimental officer. With his keenness on reading, the close friendships he had made with able young men like Purdie and Stevenson, as well as the encourage-ment he had clearly received to try for Oxford (his brief Cambridge experience might have inspired him to try there again in 1919), he was bright enough to have passed into the Staff College. Buchan's military connections might have been useful too, and perhaps Churchill's positive opinion of him.

In 1939 Alastair would be only forty-three at the outbreak of another war, perhaps still a Major or Lieutenant-Colonel. Hostilities would have given him the opportunity to rise more rapidly than in peacetime,

---

[173] Buchan and Stewart, *Scots Fusiliers*, 452.

as happened to one of his fellow 6th RSF subalterns.[174] Probably unlikely to reach the very top, as a regular soldier he was better placed for moderate distinction than Buchan's fictional "musketeer", Sir Richard Hannay. Knighthoods for Major-Generals were less likely in the second war, and certainly not for Colonels, however distinguished, as had been offered to T. E. Lawrence and rejected in 1918, though Buchan had been disappointed in his own hopes.

He once gave an address on "The Causal and the Casual in History" (the Rede Lecture for 1929), speculating on the might-have-beens in great events but for some quirky turn of fortune. Alastair's survival is one of those small historical speculations in which a casual piece of shrapnel may have inhibited the causal fulfilment of his abilities. Though with great sadness in this case, Buchan would have appreciated that since it was a favourite theme of his. Certainly one cannot imagine Alastair in a lifetime of accountancy after his taste of military life.[175]

In the next chapter we address an even more important question about the future. Dylan Thomas

---

[174] The South African, Edmund Hakewill Smith (1896-1986), was a Major in 1939, but a Major-General by the end of 1943. After retiring from the army in 1949 he was later knighted for service in the Royal Household: decorations - KCVO, CB, CBE, MC.

[175] Another example is his short story called "The Company of the Marjolaine."

powerfully poses it for us.

Have you built your ship of death, O have you?
build your ship of death, for you will need it.

Though it is wise to face up to this event even in normal times, this becomes an urgent matter amid the slaughter of war. Especially is this so when seen on the scale in which it overwhelmed the Buchans, and many who were known to them. Thomas believed that his craft was destined for oblivion. Unlike some, he and they were very well prepared before they set out. The Buchans had built their own ship of death years earlier, but it would be sailing to a very different destination. They had used it already effectively to good purpose over their sister Violet, their father, and their brother William, and would do so now with Alastair, just as he had done. They believed him to be safe in the desired, even longed for, harbour to which he had so prematurely embarked before them. They were convinced that they would surely follow in his wake when the tide was right for them to sail too, and under the same Captain, who would not fail them either.

CHAPTER THIRTEEN

ALASTAIR'S EPITAPH

In a sense Alastair's epitaph can be traced back to his father's lines received when he was nine and spending the summer at Broughton and Peebles. It was sent from Queen Mary Avenue on the 5th August 1903, a year after they had returned from their locum in South Africa.[176]

A Rhymed Letter
I'm glad to hear that you're so good,
And will be pleased to hear you're better;
And now while I'm in the mood
I'll answer your delightful letter.
You ask me – Are the roses out?
Yes, white ones, and a red one too!

---

[176] The original is in NLS Acc.11627/37. Though entitled "To Alastair, aged 8", that birthday had been in June 1902, probably on the way home from South Africa (Buchan, U., *Beyond*, 83). Apparently in response to a letter just receive, it is curious that his father did not send it until several weeks after his ninth birthday. He cannot have misdated his letter by a year, because Buchan "the absent member" sailed from Cape Town on the 19th August 1903, which fits with him being expected home soon (see next page, line 14). The anomalies cannot be explained simply by Mr Buchan's vagueness. Anna printed it in *Alastair Buchan*, 5-6. "Mohry" is a misprint for "Mhory".

Nasturtiums and candytuft
And speedwell with its spikes of blue.
Sweet-peas are coming one by one,
And Walter's seeds will soon be blowing;
The grass has grown with rain and sun,
And I am rather tired with mowing.
And Willie's taken his degree,
And John is coming in September,
And Mother thinks how glad she'll be
To welcome home the absent member.
Now, Mohry dear, your brothers all,
Each in his sphere is shaping fairly,
All loyal they to duty's call
As Highlandmen were to Prince Charlie.
And you, I'm sure will do your part,
And bear you well in school and college,
With worthy projects in your heart
And mind alert with wit and knowledge.
And better still: I hope you'll take
The gift God gives us in His pity,
So when you leave this earthly state
You'll enter yonder golden city.

One cannot doubt that Alastair fulfilled those hopes, and that Mr Buchan would have echoed the lines which the parents of his son's friend, Stevenson, chose for his war grave in France.

HE WAS SUCH A ONE AS EVERY FATHER WOULD WISH HIS SON TO BE

However, the Buchans chose something specifically Biblical for his Commonwealth War Graves Commission headstone in the Duisans Cemetery near Arras. It bears the inscription:

LENGTH OF DAYS FOR EVER

It is a rather curious to have chosen this text taken from *Psalm* 21:4: "He asked life of Thee, and Thou gavest it him, even length of days for ever and ever," In context it seems to refer solely to the King, David. The issue in the commentaries is whether this verse is to be understood as him living in his posterity, so that an allusion to the eternal kingdom of the Messiah is not to be forced on the passage. If so, it does not make sense on Alastair's grave since it was also true of him that *those who would have been, their sons, they gave, their immortality.*"[177] However, any interpretation of the verse must take account of other *Psalms* of David, most famously of the 23rd, which ends, *I shall dwell in the house of the Lord for ever.* That sounds very like "length of days for ever and ever."

However, there is an alternative, and more conservative, interpretation that "The Spirit of prophecy rises from what related to the king, to that which is peculiar to Christ; none other is blessed for ever, much less a blessing for ever."[178] It seems that

---

[177] Taken from Rupert Brooke's poem, *The Dead.*
[178] Though quoted from *Matthew Henry's Commentary* (1706-1710), this proleptic interpretation has continued to be well

only if the Buchans took it in that specifically Christian sense, meaning in, and with, Christ for ever can it make sense as an epitaph here. What is certain is that they will have given careful thought to what was chosen. Probably the words appealed because they expressed what they firmly believed was true of him eternally.

As with this chosen epitaph, Buchan was rather prone to express his deepest beliefs by suggestion rather than by explicit reference. It probably made for better poetry. Especially in the third part of his memorial elegy he refers by allusion to his assurance that Alastair has entered eternal life in Heaven: *a spirit... most ripe for immortality*; again *That just beyond our senses' veil You dwell unseen* in *Joy which no languid years can pale*; though sorrowing with *those mortal thoughts that crave For sight of those who men call dead*, he ended with the clear allusion to the Biblical affirmation that "those who believe in [Christ] should not perish, but have everlasting life". (Jesus in *St. John's Gospel*, 3:16)

I knew you moved in ampler powers,
A warrior in a purer strife,

---

known in evangelical circles ever since. It accords with such statements as that attributed to Jesus: "God so loved the world, that he gave his only begotten Son, that whosoever believeth in him should not perish, but have everlasting life." *St John's Gospel*, 3:16. It is a verse that Buchan took literally, *Presbyterianism*, 8.

Walking that world that shall be ours
When death has called us dead to life.

In the same way, his father hoped that after leaving *this earthly state*, Alastair would *enter yonder golden city*. Anna's book will have been shared for approval with her mother and his siblings before publication. Buchan's poem similarly affirmed the belief of the surviving family that their father's hope had become a reality. Though they visited the grave in that "corner of a foreign field", such is faith that they knew what mattered of their beloved Alastair was not lying there but risen, for in his case *death has called us dead to life*, and they did not doubt where he had gone.

Nevertheless, it was especially tragic that an exceptionally attractive young man gave his life before ever reaching his prime, or being able to use his gifts to the full, and realise his promise. There were others such. Although the circumstances may be very different, to lose one's life in the service of one's country is an equally great sacrifice for anyone. Moreover, Alastair and all of his immediate peers were volunteers, not conscripts. That only makes their early deaths more poignant, unless they were destined for "length of days for ever." Buchan, and his siblings could see beyond their mourning to expectancy.

CHAPTER FOURTEEN

THE HOUSE OF AUCHMACOY

32. Major General Thomas Buchan,
Colonel-in-Chief of Mar's Regiment
and later Commander-in-Chief of the
Jacobite troops in Scotland 1689-1690

These two chapters may seem to be somewhat rogue
asides to those readers uninterested in family versions

of their history and in heraldry. They may wish to move on to the conclusion of the book which really starts on 169 "Those who have reached thus far….".

Edward, Prince of Wales wrote that the Buchans "had old family connections with the regiment [The Royal Scots Fusiliers]." They trace their origins to the regiment first raised in 1678 by the fifth Earl of Mar as Colonel and known by his name. Four years later Thomas Buchan (1641-1724) was promoted to become Lieutenant-Colonel of the regiment. Born on the brink of the Civil War, his parents were strongly Royalist in sympathy. As a younger son he needed to make his own way which he did by entering the armies of France and then served in The Netherlands. To further his advancement under the later Stuarts he converted to Roman Catholicism through his nephew who had renounced his succession to the estate to become a Jesuit. James II recalled Thomas to Scotland in 1682 to help with "the suppression of lawlessness" (i.e. the activities of the Covenanters), and this will explain the military role he was given. Then in 1686, he succeeded Mar as Colonel.

Beyond his portrait, we have little idea what he was like. Among the Covenanters, he was known for "enforcing harsh laws, but not exceeding them" as many did. On the other side, an Episcopalian said of him that he was "a man eminent for courage and ancient honesty." His military failures were due to being over-hasty it is said. He was a married man with children.

In the year that Thomas was appointed to his lieutenancy, some of the regiment were issued with fusils, an early kind of grenade. They later took their name from this kind of weaponry.[179]

These Auchmacoy Buchans were long descended (and still are as Chiefs of the Clan) on their estate in Aberdeenshire, landward of the coast south of Peterhead and near Ellon. They had been proprietors there at least since 1445, and "cherished an imaginary descent" from the old Comyn Earls of Buchan, who had links with royalty, but to whom the later family had no lineal connection.[180]

After the flight of James II in 1689, Thomas served him in Ireland, where he was defeated at the battle of Windmill Hill. In the following year he came to Scotland promoted to be the Major-General and Commander-in-Chief of the Jacobite army. He was again defeated on the braes of Cromdale by troops loyal to William and Mary. After such military failures, he remained constant to the Stuarts, and spent years as a rebel fugitive between France and Scotland. His younger brother, John, had served in his regiment but remained a Protestant and was in the service of

---

[179] Most of these facts are gleaned from Buchan and Stewart, *Scots Fusiliers*, and the article in the *Oxford Dictionary of National Biography*, Volume 8.
[180] Ibid.

William and Mary. Like many Scottish families in troubled times they guarded their backs and Thomas handed over his assets to John to avoid confiscation.

Even after an amnesty allowed him home in 1703, he continued to plot for the cause. He took only a minor part in the 1715 Rebellion, but was not prosecuted, and retired to his wife's property at Ardlogie in Fyvie, where he died.[181] A significant figure, Buchan writes rather fully of his exploits in his *History* of the RSF, and some of the Peebles family claimed kinship with him and the rest of that noted house. [182]

What is the point of this Chapter in a book about Alastair? There are two questions which may seem obscure to some, but to others are of interest. The one is to ask whether Alastair had any military background in his family to spur on his early enthusiasm to be a soldier. We can discount the Peebles family. Uncle Willie used to go out locally with the Volunteers (Territorials), brother William with the Bihar Light Horse, and Uncle Thomas (so suitably baptised), over age at fifty-five in 1916, and with dyed hair, did non-combatant duties briefly in France in 1917.[183] Buchan

---

[181] Entry in the *Oxford Dictionary of National Biography.*

[182] Buchan and Stewart, *Scots Fusiliers*, 15-22, but especially 16. Much of the information in these paragraphs comes from these two books, this and the *ODNB.*

[183] Buchan, W., *Memoir*, 61; Smith, *John Buchan*, 41n; Buchan, U., "W.H.B.", 13; Lee, in "Thomas" corrects the family myths.

was loosely attached as a trooper to the Rand Rifles, claimed to have been shot at,[184] and was known as "Colonel" but for service later which was non-combatant because of his poor health. These seem to have been the only military figures in the family, and they were only briefly soldiers. Buchan surmised that had his brother, William, survived he would have found some way to serve in the Great War, but that supposes that he could obtain release from valuable Government work in India.

The other question is coupled to the first. Though Buchan rightly used his grandfather's coat of arms, he was not convinced of a supposed link with the baronial family of Buchan of Auchmacoy. One of his sons, William (later the 3rd Baron), had no such doubts and took the contrary view. Both wrote about it a little.[185] However, the claim that the family were lineally connected to the Auchmacoys would certainly link them with long dead military forebears like Colonel Thomas, or other earlier ones. There is some interest in examining that possibility.

Over sixty years ago I was an enthusiastic member of the Heraldic and Genealogical Society at university, and I still retain a sensitivity which may be activated about such matters. The late Victorian genealogist, Horace Round, was not one of my heroes but intrigued me as having a not infallible gift of

---

[184] Buchan, U. *Beyond*, 81-82.
[185] Buchan, J., *Memory-Hold-the-Door*; Buchan, W., *Memoir*.

exposing false claims. When it comes to the family of Alastair Buchan, I am not suggesting that a lineal connection with the baronial family of Buchan of Auchmacoy is unfounded. It is simply that it has been put into the public domain without, in my view, providing sufficient information to justify the pedigree. It is not yet clear whether the claim of a link with Auchmacoy is false or simply deficiently attested.

It was certainly in the mind of the first John Buchan of Peebles (1811-1883), who was Buchan's grandfather. He named his third son, Alexander Stewart (Stuart), doubtless after the Earl of Buchan, the "Wolf of Badenoch" (1343-1405), and his fourth son, Thomas, perhaps after the Jacobite commander we celebrate. Otherwise, I have seen four sources for this claim. Sub-headings may assist the reader here.

1. Source: Buchan's stated view:

Writing this at the end of his life, Buchan sees a link as a family romance rather than a fact,:

Like most Scottish families we [children] believed ourselves to be gently born. A certain John Buchan, a younger son of the ancient Aberdeenshire house of Auchmacoy, came south at the beginning of the seventeenth century and was supposed to have founded our branch. There was a missing link in the chain, and an austere antiquary like my uncle [Willie, the Town Clerk,

known hereafter on all occasions as Uncle
Willie] would never admit that the descent was
more than high probability; but we children
accepted it as proven fact, and rejoiced that
through Auchmacoy we could count kin back to
the days of William the Lion. So in the high story
of Scotland we felt a proprietary interest. [186]

It is helpful that he continues by referring to
individuals.

A Countess of Buchan (with whom we had no
conceivable connection) had crowned Robert the
Bruce; an Earl of Buchan as Constable of France
had avenged the death of Joan of Arc; a Buchan
of Auchmacoy had fallen at Flodden beside the
King; another [Thomas of whom we treat] had
led the Jacobite remnant after the death of
Dundee [John Graham of Claverhouse].

Some of this results from confused oral family lore,
which being a romance would not worry Buchan.

---

[186] Buchan, J., *Memory-Hold-the-Door*, 45; Carswell in *Wife
and friends*, 166, describes Buchan's foible in including among
pictures, hanging on the walls at Elsfield, a number of ancient
noble Buchans with whom he had no lineal connection,
including a commissioned copy of a portrait by Raeburn of the
eleventh Earl of Buchan (1742-1829) who died without issue!
& a photo of the ancestral House of Auchmacoy, Buchan, W.
John Buchan, 15 to which he had no proven link.

Hereafter the heraldic vocabulary is used in italics, with
a modern English equivalent in brackets.

2. Source: Uncle Willie's Arms 1895

Uncle Willie applied to the Lord Lyon King of Arms in January 1895 for the grant of a *coat-of-arms* in the name of his father. Then a year later, a version of the Auchmacoy sunflower was sanctioned to replace the original *crest* (distinguishing symbol on the helmet), adding a certain resemblance to their armorial *bearings* (design) on the shield. Buchan was still at home in 1894-95 and would have discussed all this questioning of the family background with his uncle before the grant of *arms* was made, and the *crest* was changed. Willie was a worthy person in his own right to apply for *arms* and did not need to prove the Auchmacoy connection in order to do so.

When properly registered, Buchan was entitled to use these *arms* himself, as were his uncles and his siblings as long as they were properly *differenced* for *cadency* (the art of differentiating others in the family from the Head). Buchan made correct use of the *arms* "in various guises" yet he remains equivocal, for we have just seen (note 186) lingering hints of a link with a more distinguished past. Romance trumped fact. In this he was rather like his early scholarly mentor in Peebles, Professor John Veitch (whose surname was the same as that of the baronial family of Dawyck mentioned by Buchan in *John Burnet of Barns*, and to whom he believed there was a missing link in his own family.) He, nevertheless, wore the Dawyck *arms* on his seal, and was known as "My dear Dawyck". [187]

We now come to a view which is rejecting of any romance and solely determined to assert a fact.

3. Source: William Buchan's Understanding

The other two sources describe the claim as factual. Insofar as these derive from Buchan's second son William, (to be distinguished from others as later the 3rd Baron), who had no doubts, they allow that the Peebles family were granted the use of the Auchmacoy arms. This belief is largely because he misinterpreted the grant of a *coat-of-arms* to Uncle Willie. It must be made quite plain that the Town Clerk obtained these in the name of his father who had died a dozen years before 1895. For this reason the *arms* became patrimonial, so that the Reverend John inherited the plain *arms* from his father, as Buchan did and the other descendants, like Uncle Willie, could bear them when properly *differenced*.

> The link must, in fact, have been satisfactorily dealt with because the austere antiquary [Uncle Willie] applied to the Lyon Court (the highest heraldic authority in Scotland) in 1895 for leave to use the arms of Auchmacoy, and these were granted to him only slightly *differenced*.[188]

---

[187] Bryce, M., *Veitch*, 162 for the Professor..
[188] Buchan, W., *Memoir*, 78.

Thus writes, William, Buchan's second son. There are doubtful matters here which will be discussed below. We shall find that the use of the Auchmacoy *arms* was not sanctioned, and he is wrong about the *crests*.

William's children recognised that he could be factually inaccurate about various things. Uncle Willie also appropriated the Auchmacoy *motto*, a quotation from Virgil meaning "Not following meaner things."

Non inferiora secutus

In adopting this there is no hidden significance, and it is not a necessary part of *arms*. Within reason, anyone is free to use whatever *motto* they wish. It is not so with shields.

In its various meanings the motto caused some amusement to his great-nephew, William (3rd Baron), who liked the "less moral, more worldly sense as going for the top."[189] He went on further to relate that,

> For many generations after John Buchan the first had left Auchmacoy, thought to have gone as the Master of the Horse to King James IV at Stirling… that particular lot of Buchans lived on in Stirlingshire, at a place called Ribbald of Polmaes, getting some sort of a living [as]… gentlemen who had little but their pride to sustain them: their pride and their brains.[190]

---

[189] Buchan, W., *Memoir*, 78.
[190] Ibid., 79.

Some of this is also inaccurate.

4. Source: Malcolm Golin's article.[191]

  This account is particularly significant here for Golin's discussion of the *arms* of both Buchan families, and the inclusion of further comments from William and his son James. So it must be made clear that Golin's purpose is not to discuss the veracity of the link with Auchmacoy, but only to reveal more about the heraldic nature of the bearings on the Tweedsmuir *arms* and the views of William and one of his sons. In doing so he is not convinced of the heraldic accuracy upon which these claims are made.

  About the Stirlingshire Buchans he adds:

> Lord Tweedsmuir is still in possession of a legal document dated 1630 and entitled "The *Testament Testamentar of John Buchan in Mains of Eisher* [Easter] *Polmais.*"

He then quotes James Buchan as saying that his grandfather's Uncle Willie

> set about proving that his offshoot of the Buchan clan descended directly from a younger son of the house of Auchmacoy, who had gone to seek his fortune at The Scottish Court, then in Stirling. [192]

  We must note that the third Baron errs in saying that "the link must, in fact, have been satisfactorily

---

[191] Golin, "Buchan's Heraldry".
[192] Ibid., 27.

dealt with" by Uncle Willie (above, 152) and his son to say that "he set about proving" (154). Buchan, who knew him well, is clear that there was still a missing link, and that Uncle Willie "would never admit that the descent was more than high probability." (above, 150) There is more to say in the next chapter about the lack of any proof that the missing link has been resolved.

However, these more recent quotations are interesting because they seem to bring together Buchan's belief in the ancestral migration to Stirling in the "early Seventeenth century" and William's statement that the first there was "the Master of the Horse to James IV" (153) in the sixteenth century. This would be that Buchan, son of Auchmacoy who , it is said, "had fallen at Flodden [1513] beside the King" (Buchan, 150 above). The two accounts, which can be compared from pages 149-150 and 152-153, may not be contradictory if the courtier's line died with him, and the Auchmacoy family were not represented in the Stirling area again for another hundred years. The truth of these matters is yet unresolved, and evidence will be presented that may show them to be other harmless and romantic myths, such as all families tend to possess.

CHAPTER FIFTEEN

THE EVIDENCE FROM HERALDRY

The discussion in this Chapter is developed from the last and the guiding headings continue.

5. The Significance of the Link and the Heraldry

In her writings Buchan's widow shows that she was much interested in genealogical matters. His own doubts about the link with Auchmacoy were posthumously still being expressed by writers who were close to her and must reflect her own understanding. This can be well illustrated by the conclusion to one of her initiatives to preserve her husband's memory.

Three years after Buchan's death, when his memory was still fresh in the minds of family and friends, Catherine Carswell was invited to Elsfield by his widow, Lady Tweedsmuir. "By the desire and with the help of the people who had lived closest to him", she arranged his papers chronologically and then was asked to "search out as best I might the pith of his mind in all the words that had been written from first to last by, to, and about him." Thereafter she helped Lady Tweedsmuir publish two books about her late husband. They collaborated well together over a couple of years. [193] The first volume was composed of selections from Buchan's writing, the second is essays, some quoted from elsewhere, others written for the book, but all created as tributes.

Curious about whether there was really any connection between these Buchans and those of Auchmacoy, she raised this question very directly with the family. Her conclusion was that if so, then surely Buchan would have made it clear in his *History of the Royal Scots Fusiliers*, published in memory of Alastair. There was very good reason for this supposition, for in his Preface, the Prince of Wales, as Colonel-in-Chief, wrote that the author "has old family connections with the regiment." It is true that he got the idea from somewhere, not necessarily from Buchan, but possibly as hearsay from someone in the regiment, and can only have meant Colonel Thomas, his brother John, and his two nephews all mentioned in the book. While one side of Buchan's split personality concerning the Jacobite/Covenanter divide would acclaim the Colonel, the loyal Jacobite, the other will have approved of the Colonel's brother, Lieutenant-Colonel John, equally believed by William to be related to the later Buchans. This John supported

---

[193] The first book was Tweedsmuir, S., *The Clearing House.* The second was Tweedsmuir, S, *Wife and Friends*; ibid., 151, 165. Carswell did the editing between January 1944 and November 1945, three months before she died: ibid, 146-147; Pilditch, *Catherine Carswell*, 169-170, & *Selected Letters*, 362.

William and Mary, together with the Presbyterian
Church settlement, the Union, and fighting in the
defeat of the Jacobites at Killiecrankie in 1715.[194]

It is also true that Buchan let the Prince's claim
be printed. It would have been difficult to challenge
his future King once the Preface had been graciously
written and received, and hard to contradict him in the
"Author's Note". Best to let it be with, elsewhere, his
own account of things, sometimes romantic rather
than strictly factual. Anyway, he made no reference to
the claim when referring to his own brother in the
book, and we have seen that it is equally certain that
he doubted it at the end of his life.

Carswell was puzzled by all this. She was
surprised by some of the pictures he displayed at
Elsfield. Others have also mentioned that they
included a photograph of Auchmacoy House and a
framed portrait of an old Earl of Buchan.[195] These
accorded with the romance if not with the proven facts.
She should not have been at all surprised that Buchan
used the *arms* attributed to his grandfather by Uncle
Willie. We shall see that these were legitimate without
having any Auchmacoy connection.

Carswell's conclusion is clear, and was
doubtless approved by his widow, that for Buchan "the
value and the operative force [of the claim] lay not in
fact but in the incomputable power of fancy." Like

---

[194] Buchan, J., *Scots Fusiliers*, 16n.
[195] See above 150, note186.

Alexander the Great, who came to believe that he was "somehow descended from Ammon", a god of Egypt, she believed that Buchan generated "action continually from romance."[196] We have already seen him still at home in 1895, and he would surely have known the circumstances in which the grant of *arms* was made. For quite different reasons, Janet Adam Smith continued to be still doubtful after she had spoken with the family in the early 1960s.[197]

The other place to look for any pedigrees and *coats-of-arms* might be in *Burke's Landed Gentry*. However, the Auchmacoy entry there does not seem hopeful. Their published record knows nothing of one who came south in the early seventeenth century. It does not record one who died at Flodden, and the Master of the Horse served in 1428-1436, eighty years earlier under James I.[198] Horace Round would have enjoyed these confusions in the family myth.

Golin identifies a greater problem about the missing link in the line between the Peebles family and the Clan Chiefs in Aberdeenshire. He quotes William making the claim that when Uncle Willie had "applied to the Lyon court... in 1895 for leave to use the *arms* of Auchmacoy... these were granted to him only slightly *differenced*" which he then explained as being

---

[196] Tweedsmuir, *Wife and Friends*, 168; cf. 150 note 186 for his pictures.

[197] Adam Smith, *John Buchan*, 1.

[198] *Burke's*, 266, 267.

"the sunflower *crest* of Buchan which for Auchmacoy, has two flowers, [but] came to Uncle Willie with one."[199]

Whatever the similarities between the *crests*, and shields William did not understand their detail. This led him into three erroneous assumptions that the link with Auchmacoy had been proven with the heralds. Firstly, he thought that evidence for this is shown by allowing the use of the sunflower *crest* by both. Then, he assumed that the heralds also sanctioned the use of the Chief's whole *arms*, and in particular the shield and *motto* as well as the *crest*. Lastly, he believed that this is clear from the use of three *erased* lions' heads by both. It can now be shown that each of these conjectures prove the opposite of what he thought.

6. Further Doubts about William's Claim

The significance of the *crest* was greatly over-emphasised by William. These additions are not an essential part of the *arms*, but only for "those who wish them."[200] At the same time he also misunderstood the Peebles *blazon* (the design described in words) which was of a single *sunflower proper*. This simply means in its natural colouring. Auchmacoy also has a single flower. It is not a double

---

[199] Buchan, W., *Memoir*, 78.
[200] Innes, *Scots Heraldry*, 35; acknowledgement is made that image 33 is adapted from Golin's "Heraldry", as are 34-36.

one, but is correctly *blazoned* as *The sun shining upon a sunflower full blown proper.* William mistook the sun to be the other part of a double flower, as was pointed out by Golin. A more careful comparison of those *blazons* would probably have revealed this to him.

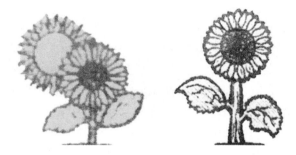

33. Crests: Auchmacoy, William's supposed double sunflower (left), & Peebles (right).

William's statements are misleading both in the eyes of a competent herald and of a discerning genealogist. For the herald the key part of a *coat-of-arms* is the shield, and the *crest* is of interest only to a far lesser degree; the reason for this being because "The shield is the foundation of everything. Some people only have a right to a shield alone, but without a shield neither *crest* nor anything else can exist."[201]

---

[201] Innes, *Scots Heraldry*, 28; Illustration 38, on 166, is adapted from Plate XX in ibid.

The reasons go back to the original purpose. The shield was of vital significance. Its design revealed the identity of the knight in command of men when he was totally clothed in armour. In battle the clansmen needed to know how, and where, to look to their Chief for orders, example, rescue if hard pressed, and commands such as when to attack or retire or to change sides as the course of the conflict progressed. Only one man could bear those exact *arms*, the Chief. True, the *charges* (symbols) on the shield of a son or brother would be in the same colouring and with the same *charges*, but *differenced* by a much smaller *charge*, specific to each.[202] These little ones were superimposed upon a larger, and were known as marks of *cadency*, universally set by the heralds.

Golin is at pains to clarify for us that the Buchan shields were *blazoned* as:

Argent three lions' heads erased sable
for Auchmacoy

Azure a fess between three lions' heads erased
argent for Peebles

---

[202] The Revd Charles Boutell (1812-1877) has a whole chapter on English *cadency*. He accepts that in earlier times there was a method achieved "by modifying or adding to the original arms." Scott-Giles, *Boutell*, 108. Willie Buchan applied in Scotland and not in earlier times, and in any case they became "in effect an independent heraldic composition." Ibid.

Left to Right: 34. Peebles Arms - silver
(argent) *on blue* (azure). *35. Auchmacoy Arms
- black* (sable) *on Silver* (argent) *36. Uncle
Willie's Arms - with a* fess *for difference.*

Thus, in the Peebles *arms* the shield is now in a *colour*, with the heads and a *fess* (a band across the middle), both now in a *metal* (in colouring metals are *argent* {silver} and *or* {gold}.) This has become an entirely new *coat-of-arms* in a way that is now described.

To put the two *blazons* in simple terms, Uncle Willie's shield was basically blue with silver lions' heads *erased*, two and one, between a silver band (*fess*) across the middle. In total contrast, Auchmacoy had basically a silver shield, no band, but three lions' heads in black. No Buchan clansman would have recognised Uncle Willie's shield as their own because the background colouring (*field*) was an essential part of recognition. The Peebles shield was not that of Auchmacoy. At best, it was no more than an imitation of the original in different colouring, allowed by the herald because it made no pretence at appropriating Auchmacoy. The addition of the band (*fess*) is interesting only as the chosen addition of a new charge. Though there is no evidence of the link with Auchmacoy having been made, it might seem that the heralds went out of their way to accommodate the romance of the connection, but not the fact. But did they? Were they making an individual exception or following standard practice?

My understanding is the latter, and this also explains why what William took to be confirmation of the lineal link was actually a denial of it. In Scotland only one *armiger* of a particular name may bear the plain *arms*. In the case of those with the Buchan name this is obviously Auchmacoy. Any proven kinsman of his can bear those same *arms* as long as they are properly *differenced*. Other unrelated people of that name may legally bear *arms* derived by some means from the original but *differenced* in a form other than that used by his family for *cadency,* and *charges* may be added.[203]

In my view this is exactly what the heralds granted to Uncle Willie. He took the three *erased*

---

[203] In Scotland it has been a known practice for associated families, even of a different surname, to have based their legitimate arms on using similar colouring and *charges* to those of their feudal overlord. There is the instance of eleven Renfrew families, all with different surnames, basing their arms on the *fess chequy* of the Stewarts, their feudal superiors, perhaps because of "positions held within the Steward's household." Malden, "Heraldic Hierarchy".

heads from Auchmacoy but *differenced* them in two ways not used by the family: first by changing the colouring of the *field* and *charges*, and secondly by including a *fess* as the new *charge*. Thus, he was in no way being granted the use of the Auchmacoy family *arms* only "slightly differenced". In fact, the grant of *arms* secured by Uncle Willie for his father shows that he was not related to the Chief by blood, but only shared the same surname.

37. Martlet

7. A Minor Complication

Alastair was eligible to bear the Peebles *arms*, *differenced* with the small *charge* of a martlet for the fourth son, centred on the larger *charge* of a *fess*. This is an heraldic bird akin to the swallow, and the name may mean "little martin". Then, because Uncle Willie was not his father's eldest son, he still had to *difference* for *cadency*. This brings us to another curiosity about Uncle Willie's own shield. *Cadency* was done with the added *charge* of a *fess*, but this is *engrailed*, that is with wavy edges. I do not understand why the herald allowed this *difference*. It seems to

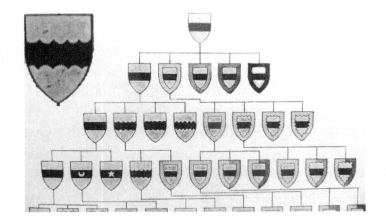

38. Plate XX: Uncle Willie's fess
engrailed *is third row, second
from the left, and inset top left.*

imply *arms* granted to his grandfather (above). Maybe
in discussion Willie preferred the *fess engrailed*
without the *bordure* and, having no heirs, it would not
be perpetuated. Alternatively, having criticised
William, I may have missed a finer point in *cadency*
myself. Had the link been proved, the heralds were
well able to find a shield, from within the labyrinth of
possibilities, to *difference* the Peebles family
appropriately from the actual Auchmacoy *arms*.

8. Conclusion

Had William been correct to say that the
Auchmacoy *arms* were granted only slightly
differenced, Uncle Willie would have borne a silver
shield with black heads, and some mark of *cadency*, in

Scotland likely to be a *bordure* round the edge in sharp contrast to the silver. Clansmen would have recognised him as of the Auchmacoy family but not their Chief. So those elements which William took to be proofs that the missing link had been found are no such thing. This includes the Polmais *Testament Testamentar* which tells us that some Buchans were living there in 1630; but how does it link them to Auchmacoy? Were they actually ancestors of the Peebles family, and if so how? As yet we have no answers. As for the sunflower *crest*, it indicates nothing apart from the satisfaction of a romantic notion. Many different families bore the same or similar *crests*, and anyway in the beginning only tournament knights were granted them. The shield is the essence of the *arms*, though people often speak of it loosely and erroneously as the *crest*.

Though all this does question William's basic belief that the missing link had been found, it does not prove him wrong. Perhaps it has been discovered, but he provides us only with assumption, not with proof. Neither he, nor anyone else to my knowledge, has identified a link and proved in print that the succeeding generations were actually lineally connected to Auchmacoy.

Consistent with this lack of proof is the Tweedsmuir lineage in *Burke's Peerage* for 1939, the last before Buchan died. It begins no further back than Buchan's grandfather, that John Buchan who had become established in Peebles. It is he who migrated there, founded the legal firm which successive generations ran for a century, and posthumously in whose name the *arms* were granted. The lack in *Burke* of any link with Auchmacoy is also an indication that Buchan himself did not believe this to exist. He would temperamentally have preferred the satisfaction of possessing a longer lineage[204]. Indeed it is surprising that the one in *Burke* does not descend from the Polmais Buchans. Did he doubt this, too? It is the same in the *Burke's Landed Gentry* 2001 edition, at the time when William shared information with Golin. If the link had been proved by then surely the lineage would have been extended to include Polmais, and the rich harvest of ancestral personalities from Auchmacoy?

Though it may seem slightly surprising to us, the old lawyer is described there as "Buchan of Skellknowe", that small estate of twenty acres at Leadburn which he owned for little more than a dozen years before the Bank failure forced him to sell it. Nevertheless, in Scottish custom he was no doubt briefly the Laird of Skellknowe, rather than just "Buchan, burgher of Peebles".

If the Peebles family were so sure of an Auchmacoy connection, why did they not persuade the editors to include it in the entry? Similarly, one would have considered that the Auchmacoys might be

---

[204] Adam Smith, *John Buchan*, 347-351 for a discussion of his supposed snobbery.

happy to embellish their record by including "ancestor of the Barons Tweedsmuir of Elsfield" as they have done with other such progenitors of cadet families thought to be worthy of such recognition.

I accept that none of this proves that William was wrong to believe the link was made. It is just that the evidence of a link has not been made public. What is needed is to have proven identity of the individuals who made the link between the two families and when this was. Then sceptics would be confounded.

Those who have reached this far may well feel that I have made heavy weather of a trivial matter. Ursula Buchan, who is an ever constant source of enlightenment, glosses over it without comment, apart from adding that Buchan was proud of having the grant of arms, and perhaps Alastair was also. The "doodles" in his common-place book suggest that.[205] Being an *Armiger* may have made Buchan feel more secure when he went up to Oxford a few months later and would meet the armorially endowed heirs to ancient peerages like "Algy" Wyndham (later Lord Leconfield) and "Bron" (soon to be Lord) Lucas. Moreover, he could quarter them with Ebury, suitably *differenced*, when he married Susan Grosvenor.[206]

There is no evidence that Alastair moved in such circles, although William in India had proposed

---

[205] Buchan, U., *Beyond*, 34.
[206] Golin, "Buchan's Heraldry", 31 for the engraved silver coffee pot.

to a Cluny Macpherson of ancient lineage. If the link is directly back to the Master of the Horse, whatever reign he lived in, the Price of Wales's reference to a family connection will still then have been pretty remote. If the Polmais family were directly descended from a later Auchmacoy younger son, a three hundred year interval is a long time for the martial genes to have reappeared in him.[207] In that sense Alastair seems to have been his own man.

I have merely scratched the surface of this matter, being unable to give it exhaustive treatment. That must be left to another. Suffice it to say that over the missing link, as far as I have discovered, the present representatives of his "race and name" are for Buchan against his son William, the third Baron. Being no expert as herald, genealogist or academic, it is not for someone like me to judge. Whether Alastair had this distinguished regimental connection, I will leave it to readers more qualified to decide, or some one of them to prove.

There is one other aspect to all this which relates to Alastair. Although Catherine Carswell did not believe in the lineal link with Auchmacoy and military ancestors, there is a better way to end here than with questionable connections to baronial families. Rather than just the missing link, she gave us her conclusion about noble traits of character in anyone.

---

[207] Fictionally, Buchan liked such reappearances, cf. *The Path of the King*, Peter Pentecost in *The Blanket of the Dark*.

Buchan had corresponded a little with her husband over his writing, and less so with her. He helped them financially when they were struggling Scottish authors. She only met him once, at his request when, without prior warning, he asked to be allowed to become a kind of Godfather to their only son. Less than four years younger than Buchan, she had also grown up in a deeply committed Free Church Glasgow family and having grandfathers on both sides as ministers. Her own escape from her perceived bonds of this shared background in the same city had led to very different results: "his tastes in men and books had seemed to be as contrary to mine as were his politics."[208] With some uncertainty, she approached her lunchtime appointment, but was surprised by his personality and he completely won her over.

She came to this conclusion later, after having gone through his papers at the request of his widow.

If John Buchan had not noble blood in his veins – and, for all I know, he had – his pulses were supplied in the manner proper to great nobles. His conscience was tender, his performance exemplary, his scutcheon without stain. As another friend has said of him, a friend who knew him far better than I, he was "a verray parfyt knight."[209]

---

[208] Tweedsmuir, *Wife and Friends*, 155.
[209] Ibid., 170-171.

The full quotation from the General Prologue to Chaucer's *Canterbury Tales* includes the word "gentil" after "parfyt". To gloss it over in a rough rendering into Modern English, which might be erroneously given as "a very, perfect, gentle knight", does not do justice to the original. The Middle English has more of the sense that he was "a truly perfect knight of noble character." She quoted something else said about him which is equally true, and the very key to his character: "He was a supremely honest Christian gentleman, whose faith was simple, unshakable and inspired."[210] He did not need the Auchmacoy link to be "gentil" (noble) in that medieval sense.

The same could be said of Alastair.

Grateful acknowledgement is made to Dr Golin
for his comments on the Buchan *crests*.

Endnote on Romance and Scandal

Some readers may ask why there has been no word of romance or scandal to liven up this account of an Edwardian youth.[211] The reason is that I have found no hint of either. Moreover, we have seen the judgment of his peers, not just his family. They

---

[210] Tweedsmuir, *Wife and Friends*, 170-171.

[211] Anthony Quinn criticises a better book by another because, "in a life apparently unshadowed by scandal or dishonour, what might have lent a dash of vinegar was some deep-lying flaw in…character", and "without redeeming vices it is very dull to read." *Sunday Times*, 7th April 2019

knew him, we did not, and must accept their conclusions. No one would suppose that all such youths were pure but there are good reasons for this assessment in his case. For most boys in their teens at that time education was single-sex. They lived in a largely all-male world then, and some like Alastair continued to do so at university. This was still true for many in my own youth. There was only one girl ever seen at our lectures in the Old History School. From such a world Alastair was plucked, at the early age of twenty, straight into the even more all-male world of war. Apart from at church and other brief social occasions there was little opportunity for him to mix with girls. His father married in his late twenties, and John and William did not propose until their early thirties. As for Walter, he lived his life in the female companionship of his mother and Anna, to both of whom he was devoted. These were Alastair's role models, and not unusual.

Besides there was a wider restraint. It is so well known that shows at the Windmill Theatre near Piccadilly Circus were adapted, as late as 1932, so that young men without experience should at least see a female body, admittedly at a distance and still-life, before they died in battle. Moreover, many like Alastair were schooled in the Christian view of marriage between one man and one woman to the exclusion of all others. Alastair came from a family where poetry was widely quoted around the table, and they loved Tennyson. He will have known, as I did at the age of fifteen and taught by an old lady in her eighties,[212] what Arthur expected of his knights:

> *To break the heathen and uphold the Christ,*
> *To ride abroad redressing human wrongs,*

---

[212] Mrs Florence Whiting (c.1870-c.1956). Her husband's father died leaving the family firm in debt. He worked for years before he cleared it all and only then proposed. As a result they were too late to have children.

To speak no slander, no, nor listen to it,
To honour his own word as if his God's,
To lead sweet lives in purest chastity,
To love one woman only, cleave to her,
And worship her by years of noble deeds
Until they won her; for indeed I knew
Of no more subtle master under heaven
Than is the maiden passion for a maid,
Not only to keep down the base in man,
But teach high thought, and amiable words,
And courtliness, and the desire of fame,
And love of truth, and all that makes a man.[213]

For a better world, it would seem that Alastair made a fair stab at doing this. As for romance, his time and opportunity had not yet come.

---

[213] From "King Arthur's Farewell to Queen Guinevere" in "The Idylls of the King".

39. Alastair: framed portrait in oils by Sir William Orpen, RA, on loan to the John Buchan Story, Peebles, 2020, (by kind permission).

CHAPTER SIXTEEN

ENVOI: A NOTE ON DUTY

Perhaps the most startling passage in this book, and the most incomprehensible to many, is on page 96, quoting what the Chaplain wrote to the family about Alastair saying

> I thought it might be some comfort to you to know that I believe he was ready to meet his Maker for whose cause he was soon to give his life, 'filling up what was behind in the sufferings of Christ.'

To those readers it must seem a very odd thing to have thought, so that it poses the questions why did he say it? and what could he mean? The phrase comes from the New Testament, in St Paul's *Letter to the Colossians* 1:24, and there is no doubt that the family will have understood and appreciated the comment. They were steeped in the Bible. Mr Buchan had probably preached on the verse, and his children had imbibed an interest in St Paul from him. Certainly, he will have been much talked about in home and church. Buchan hoped to write a book about this apostle after he had left Canada in 1940 (see below 179, note 215).

When *In Memoriam The Reverend John Buchan 1847-1911* was published in 1912, the initials

A B (for Anna) appear there on page 19. This is followed by forty pages of his poems, as well as appreciations of the man by three former colleagues. The bulk of the book, however, is filled with two hundred and eighty pages which include seven of his sermons, as well as fifteen theological addresses on "The Apostolic Evangel". Buchan's hand can be seen in all these additions, revealing how they wanted their father to be remembered. A consideration of them is helpful in revealing what they especially recalled of their father's preaching. It was ensured that St Paul was well represented in this carefully dated selection, and they give us a clear sense of the Christian thought world in which Buchan grew up and sought to live by. Again, we must add, and so did Alastair.

Perhaps the very last address in their father's ministry (May 1910) was delivered just as he retired and almost immediately suffered the heart attack which precluded any further preaching. It is called "What St Paul says of Himself." Because of its timing it was particularly poignant in its significance to them. A good sermon makes its main points and ends with a challenge.

Here he described St Paul's life in which he experienced his radical conversion. Having changed from being Saul, his Hebrew name, he became known as Paul, which was a Roman one. This nomenclature is important because having once been a Jewish authoritative figure he became the Christian apostle to the Roman world. Mr Buchan centres his challenge around these sharply different Jekyll and Hyde characters.

Saul boasted mainly in things of the flesh: his ancestry and upbringing, his career and importance, his wealth and comfort, his good character in keeping the Commandments. St Paul trusted in nothing but the spiritual, the salvation he felt privileged to enjoy through his trust in, and obedience (duty) to, the Risen Christ. Mr Buchan's challenge is, "Which will you be – Saul the 'Sanhedrist', a lost soul, or Paul the saint, associating with the spirits of just men made perfect, shining in the light of his Saviour?" You must decide for yourselves. Saying this, he was preaching for conversion.[214]

Put more briefly, Mr Buchan's challenge is this. Which of the two characters should a Christian seek to emulate? The choice is either Saul or St Paul.

There is a close link between duty and Christian fortitude (see 113, note 149, & below, 187) expressed by Buchan in *Mr Standfast*, where Peter Pineaar says that "the Apostle Paul was the head man at the job." Among his plans for retiring to Elsfield in 1940, necessitated by poor health, there was a book about the Apostle Paul together with other such contracts. Jim Greig observed that this desire had its basis long before. "The activity of [St.] Paul and his reaction to

---

[214] Discussed in my thesis and *John Buchan's Faith*.

the ups and downs of his career must have struck Buchan the boy just as forcibly as his theology."[215]

Here is just a bit of fun:

> *For duty, duty must be done,*
> *The rule applies to every one,*
> *And painful though that duty be,*
> *To shirk the task were fiddle-de-dee!*

This was written by W. S. Gilbert in the comic opera *Ruddigore*. Nevertheless it belies the underlying fact that the serious reality of a belief in duty ran very deeply through the society in which Alastair grew up.[216] Yes, one can disparage it as the days of the height of Empire, but the personal self-sacrifices of many for indigenous people in the worthier aspects of that cause are too little appreciated today. Duty had a very firm Christian basis in people's lives at the time. It is much to his credit that Alastair's brother William was similarly motivated in India, and died young.

---

[215] Lownie, *Presbyterian Cavalier*, 282. I had long ago read of a reference to the contracted book on St Paul, but the source eluded me. I am grateful to Ursula Buchan for pointing me to confirmation in her book *Beyond*, 404. In fact, Lownie mentions it in *Presbyterian Cavalier*, 331, cf. 282 and got it from Greig, *John Buchan Journal* 11 (Spring 1992) who does not cite the source. All three writers seem convinced of the fact.

[216] Gilbert believed in duty himself, was a keen member of the military volunteers, and died going to the rescue of a young girl in trouble bathing in his lake. A friend had asked him to give two girls a swimming lesson.

It is no surprise that Alastair's poem is full of the concept of duty to God and to others. Mr Buchan speaks of his young son's older brothers as *All loyal they to duty's call*; Buchan of *the high duty nobly done*; even the RSF soldier has the sense of fulfilled duty in seeking *the glory of God and your country, too,* and *the gift that to Honour you gave.*[217]

Recently, there has been some renewed and laudatory interest in the press regarding Captain Noel Chavasse, RAMC, the only man to win the Victoria Cross twice during the First World War. This has partly been caused by the auctioning of the schoolboy scrapbook he kept with his twin brother. He had a background steeped in Christianity. His father was a bishop and his twin would become one. As a sixteen year old he was fascinated by warfare and drew many sketches of battles. It was at the time of the South African War. Years later, and soon after he qualified, he joined the army as a doctor before the War. On one page of the scrapbook he had written, "Duty at all costs." When he was twice that age and dying of wounds he sent a message to his fiancée explaining his imminent death because "Duty called and called me to obey."[218]

As a dedicated Christian, it is an insight into belief in those days that on the 16th October 1916 he

---

[217] See above, 31-32, 139, 100, 122.
[218] "Boyhood Tales of Valour Came True for Double VC", *The Times*, 10th April 2020.

wrote this about a sudden moving experience:

> At midday I rushed off and attended Holy
> Communion in a ruined Church. There were a lot
> of men and officers there and it was really a very
> impressive sight to see them kneeling so
> reverently and expectantly to receive the
> sacrament. Really I think I have never seen men
> look more manly.[219]

Of course, duty may be inspired by any strong belief. Alastair was no more than just eighteen when he wrote his poem (see pages 31-32) declaring so clearly his own Christian sense of dedicated duty to God and to others. [220] "Each one should use whatever gift he has received to serve others, faithfully administering God's grace in its various forms." (*First Letter of Peter* 4:10). Just as Chavasse carried his own youthful ideals of duty into real war, so did Alastair

---

[219] "He who would true valour see", *The Church Times*, 1st September 2017. The article continued about Chavasse: "His favourite hymns were ... 'Just as I am' and 'Praise to the Holiest'....they both show a profound acceptance of salvation through Jesus Christ." His headmaster predicted that he would become a distinguished missionary doctor or clergyman. "In fact it is only his faith that draws together all the elements of his life...." I am bound to say that this echoes what I believe to be true of Alastair and Buchan.

[220] Examples of his dedication to the needs of others can be found above on pages 39-40, 53, 56-57, 82-83, 94, 103, 183.

with the dedication earlier expressed in his own poem where his sincerity rings true.

However, that does not tell us what the Chaplain meant by 'filling up what was behind in the sufferings of Christ.' That has to be understood in the context in which St Paul wrote it about his own sufferings (and eventual death) which he readily endured to help others to enjoy the same assurance of the Christian faith as he did.[221] A wider understanding is consistent with the teaching of Jesus about discipleship. Let us see what this means.

Clearly, in Christian teaching no one can add anything to the worth of what Jesus has already done to be our Lord and Saviour. However, Jesus must now be presented to others through the faithfulness of those who are already Christians today, otherwise that is still lacking in his sufferings. In a human sense that means being willing to sacrifice themselves to the needs, and to the good of others in a Christian way. Thereby, they are being, as far as is humanly possible, Christ-like.

We have seen that Nurse Reid quoted *St John's Gospel*, 15:13 in her condolences: "Greater love hath no man than this, that a man lay down his life for his friends."[222] Jesus first said these words about himself predicting the crucifixion. It is frequently applied to others. There was an often expressed belief at the time

---

[221] There is a close link between Christian fortitude and a Christian's duty, see 113, note 149.
[222] See note 127 on page 92.

that those who were fighting against what was seen as evil were doing Christ's work. Writing to Buchan in May, having just received Alastair's personal clothing among his effects, Anna wrote to Buchan asking "did you see the thing in the Times Lit. Sup. last week on the wooden crosses?"

It is interesting to tease out what was in Anna's mind and had caught her fancy in *The Times Literary Supplement*. The "thing" she referred to is a front page piece called "The Soldier Patriot".[223] The argument is that the British servicemen poets do not write about their sacrifices in terms of Patriotism. Rather than talking about this, it is "shadowed forth in familiar symbols" on more homely subjects including the countryside, school or college, the evocative sights and sounds, and "the dust out of which inarticulate flowers" will bloom above the new made graves. There is no hatred of the Germans, but rather a kind of sightless brotherhood:

You are blind like us, you hurt no man designed,
And no man claimed the conquest of your land.
But gropers both through fields of thought confined,
We stumble and we do not understand.

It is only at the end of the article that the literary symbol of the wooden cross is used. "Above the dust is the highest honour that has been won in any war:-"

---

[223] This was kindly found for me by Elaine Brown at the National Library of Scotland in July 2020.

Rest you content, more honourable far
Than any Orders is the cross of wood,
The symbol of self-sacrifice that stood
Bearing the God whose brethren you are.

From these war poets "the joyless non-combatant - sadly conscious that middle age, always a blunder, is now a kind of crime - may learn to be a patriot and not talk about it."[224]

One can see at once why Anna was so reminded of Alastair by all this. He too used the symbols of homely things in his letters, like a snug hotel fire, the smell of good food, the Border country, playing with Buchan's children, and especially humour. For him also, duty, patriotism, call it what you will, was summed up in his Christian poem. Written a few years later, it could have been added to Osborn's collection under the same heading.

The article expresses all that Henry Fairlie was

---

[224] The writer does not give his sources for the poems quoted, but they are easy to discover. The first is from "To Germany" by Charles Hamilton Sorley, killed at the Battle of Loos, October 1915. The second, "The Cross of Wood" by Cyril William Winterbotham, killed on the Somme in August 1916, had not been published when the article was written. It was in "The Christian Soldier" section of *The Muse in Arms* by E. B. Osborn, published in November 1917, so that with this foreknowledge the piece in the NLS was probably written by the journalist, Osborn. The British Library has confirmed this.

objecting to (see 116), and that typified the Buchans' reaction to Alastair's death. It is all the more moving as it ends up with a strong Christian allusion by a subaltern, William Winterbotham. Readers at the time will not have recognised the quotation, or known that he had already been killed. As for the Buchans, it was they that had suffered the terrible loss and they dealt with it in their own way, much as he did.

Anna was moved to add about the pocket New Testament that she found in Alastair's kit:

It was rather strange that the mark in the little Testament he had in his breast pocket when he fell lay at the words. 'He who findeth his life shall lose it, but he [who] loses his life for my sake shall find it.' (*St. Matthew's Gospel*, 10:39.)[225]

All this can be taken a little further. St Paul was very strong on Christians being in union with Christ. He is consistent with what Jesus said in places like *St. John's Gospel*, 14:20: "…you will know that I am in my Father, and you in me, and I in you." Christians suffer because they are united to Him who suffered. Their sufferings then complete His sufferings as they live out the proclaiming of the Gospel of the Cross.

Apart from anything else, it must be seen as quite something that Alastair maintained the high reputation that he did among his own contemporaries

---

[225] Anna to Buchan, Peebles, 7th May 1917, John Buchan Story Archive. Anna quotes the KJV loosely here.

and that, despite having had to help to bury his closest wartime friend, he never lost his inner happiness. He cherished the longer view, knowing that this life is not everything. It is worth recalling the most telling thing that Anna ever reported about him. "Over and over he has told us, 'Remember, I shan't mind going'." [226] It is truly exceptional that such a young man, with so much to look forward to in life, should have repeated this in a family where he was so beloved, while they were praying fervently that he would survive the War. One can see it as expressing a selfless and caring realism, as well as the undaunted assurance of his Christian conviction. He knew the dangers and did not want them to underestimate the risk. It might help them, in the event of his loss, to be positive and to match the courage they so admired in him. It did so.

The Chaplain sensed that this was how Alastair had sought to live, so he wrote to give the family assurance and consolation in their bereavement. If others do not, they would readily have understood what he wanted to say to them, and why. It was far more than Colonel Gordon, try as he manfully might, could possibly express about Alastair. Thus in quoting the words of St Paul, the Chaplain used the highest tribute he could ever pay.

*   *   *   *   *   *

---

[226] Anna to John, Peebles, 23rd June 1917. See also above 112, and Walter on 111 above.

For the reader: The book about Alastair has been concluded. These notes on attendant subjects may interest a few readers.

POSTSCRIPT

Endnote: Faith and Fortitude in the Buchan Family

The careful reader of Buchan's fictional writings will soon realise that there is within them a discrete element of commending the Christian faith. This may be found simply in the good characters who are seen to uphold Christian standards of behaviour such as honour, duty, faithfulness and sacrifice. More occasionally he will write about a specific Christian commitment as in *The Blanket of the Dark.* Then *Sick Heart River*, Buchan's "most significant late work... brings back Sir Edward Leithen, this time facing death himself, and it seems to expand on and deepen part of the final section of *The Gap in The Curtain.*"[227]

Buchan believed that in adversity classical stoicism and the stiff upper lip were insufficient of themselves. Real fortitude demanded something more, and for him it was found in the hope enshrined in his Christian faith, the bedrock of his existence. From his father's teaching he retained a belief in and respect for "conversion in its plain evangelical sense." It is "still the greatest factor in any man's life" and "there is still for every man the choice of two paths."[228] He wanted people to decide about their future for "the experience which theology calls 'conversion'... in some form or other, is the destiny of every thinking man."[229] He often challenge people to "make their soul." Their conclusion was up to them, but he was in no doubt where the truth lay.

---

[227] Kelly, "Introduction" to the Polygon edition, xiii.
[228] Buchan, J., *Presbyterianism*, 6.
[229] Buchan, J., *Oliver Cromwell*, 67.

Addressing the opening of Cathcart Church in 1925 he maintained that "within these walls human beings will fight the old fight for their soul's salvation, and will make the great decision between the broad path and the narrow path" (*St Matthew's Gospel*, 7: 13-14). He ended with the motto of Glasgow University. It quotes the words of Jesus being "the way, the truth, and the life." Buchan called them "the greatest words ever spoken in the hearing of mankind."[230] They continue: "no one comes to the father but by me." (*St John's Gospel* 14:6)

These dogmatic comments were made over a period of a dozen years, and he was equally strong in his memoirs, quoting Blake with approval that "if a man does not have the religion of Christ, he will have the religion of Satan." Some critics have accused Buchan of saying what people wanted him to tell them. [231] That won't wash here. Some of his readers, and others of his hearers at an international conference in Canada, will not necessarily have agreed with such unequivocal statements about their eternal well-being, or welcomed them. It was his testimony.

This is what he, and the other surviving Buchans, believed. We have touched on fortitude a little, and its source in the Buchans, and their coping with grief (110 & 113 above). They solaced their grieving with their Christian belief and in a brave resolve (above, 113). As I proof-read this book, a friend has written expressing admiration for one, mutually known to us both, who is overcoming bereavement in an exactly similar way. "Most of us cannot manage stoicism or a stiff upper lip but [he] can. The woke deride such Victorian approaches of course, but they also lack the faith that can carry one through the worst of life… I am glad to say he does not." Again, "CJW

---

[230] National Library of Scotland, Acc. 7214/312.
[231] Buchan, J., *Memory-Hold the-Door*, 292: Lee, "Buchan & Christian Platonism", 35.

is keeping everything together and making things easy for his friends." (Ken Brown, Archivist at Reading School, Berkshire, 25th August 2020). Faith is more than just a stiff upper lip in testing times. Buchan adopted a similar Christian role for himself and his family.

Though amid other matters like Buchan's supposed disappointment with his progress in contemporary British politics, critics have sometimes noted this emphasis in *The Gap in the Curtain*. Five men are given foreknowledge of what *The Times* will report about them in a year's time on the 10th June. For two of them it is their death. Stuart Kelly says that the one certain thing about the future is that "we will all die." "*The Gap in the Curtain* is all about this more than anything else."[232] Daniell saw clearly that "without the power of Grace, the participants simply encounter blind fate. With it, Charles Ottery came out of the Valley of the Shadow to the Delectable Mountains."[233] His pupil, Kate Macdonald, took up the point made briefly by Janet Adam Smith[234] that Ottery is the one who forgot himself. In contrast, Sir Robert Goodeve, "unable to forget himself… gives up, waiting hopelessly for his own death",[235] while Ottery "forgets himself completely" through his fear for the life of the girl he loves who becomes dangerously ill. Andrew Lownie sees deeper and mentioned wider issues like " the redemptive power of love, resurrection, and the nature of Free Will and predestination."[236] Again, Daniell saw the story as being about "the visitation of the Holy Spirit … and the assurance of the power of the Risen Christ."[237] (Buchan set the story at Whitsuntide). However, none seems to

---

[232] Kelly, "Introduction" to the polygon edition, xii.
[233] Daniell, *Interpreter's House*, 314.
[234] Adam Smith, *John Buchan*, 268.
[235] *Companion*, 81.
[236] *The Presbyterian Cavalier*, 168.
[237] *Interpreter's House*, 165.

have brought out the full Christian significance of the book, probably for lack of space. That is now attempted.

What I celebrate here is the way that Buchan introduced the spiritual with a chance remark. He followed this by building up the drama slowly through what happens, and then working it out in a particularly satisfying way. The Labour leader and Prime Minister, Sir Derrick Trant, suddenly retires saying, "Thank God it's over. Now I shall have peace to make my soul."[238] Then we are led back into the scrabbling world of ambition. Tavanger, the first man described, seeks to acquire a great business advantage, and crashes. The second, Mayot, aspires in Parliament to obtain one of the great offices of state, and fails. The third is Daker who, though consistently determined to avoid joining an expedition into the wilds of South America, is ambushed by extraordinary events and becomes desperate to go, He does so at the last minute.

The stakes are higher for the last two, for it is the announcement of their deaths which is predicted. A fatal weakness in the Goodeve family, is described as them having "spirit but not fortitude."[239] They could face the sudden onslaught of death in battle, (176), "not a trace of the white feather", but they could not endure its slow and inevitable approach. Thus, Goodeve, the young M.P. with a promising future, stoically tries to avoid his fate, but dies of fright slowly induced by his self-centredness and loss of nerve. In the event his death was completely unnecessary because the obituary appeared through an understandable misapprehension. Since he had had no hope, his death from heart failure was soon genuinely reported. A promising career which had shown spirit was extinguished by his lack of fortitude.

---

[238] Ch.III/IV/113: this, & all the latter numbers in brackets refer to *The Gap in the Curtain*, Polygon edition, note on 195 explains.
[239] Ch.V/IV/177.

The climax comes in the description of the remaining character. In Captain Charles Ottery there are strong remembrances of Alastair. He, too, served in the Scots Fusiliers, and both would eventually emerge from the "Shadow of the Valley to the Delectable mountains", the very words that a friend had written about Alastair when he died.[240] Charles was also facing the foreknowledge of his death on the same date as the others. He goes through various attempted anodynes to overcome this threat. Initially there is anger and denial. His wooing of Pamela has failed, so he tried "a kind of stoicism", then a determined return to work, sport of various kinds, a deliberately tough venture into the wilds , and "though he had never lived a life of pleasure" he now attempted to lose himself in unfamiliar hedonism. He tried gambling, drunkenness, and riding so hard when out hunting that "he made himself "a nuisance in the field." None of this brought peace, only "a doubtful name"[241] and all helps fail him. Along the way, he "reflects on the implications of death."

> His religion was of the ordinary public-school brand, the fundamentals of Christianity accepted without much comprehension. There was an after-world, of course, about which a man did not greatly trouble himself: the important thing, the purpose of religion, was to have a decent code of conduct in the present one. But now the latter did not mean much to him, since his present life would soon be over.... There were pages of the diary filled with odd amateurish speculations about God and Eternity, and once or twice there was even a kind of prayer. But somewhere in the barrens Charles seems to have decided that he better let metaphysics alone. What

---

[240] Daniell, *Interpreter's House*, 314; See 120 above, where "Delectable Mountains" is misquote as "celestial country".
[241] *Gap*, Ch.VI/II/197-201,

concerned him was how to pass the next eight months without disgracing his manhood. He noted cases of people he had known who, when their death sentence was pronounced by their doctor, had lived out the remainder of their days with a stiff upper lip, even with cheerfulness.

"The presumption is that this resolve [stoicism and a stiff lip] gave him a certain peace" concluding this stage in his agony, but "that peace did not survive his return to England."[242]

After all these stratagems have failed him,[243] he walked alone on the Devon moors, and reached rock bottom. "There was nothing before him now but a dreadful, hopeless passivity."[244] Then by chance he unexpectedly meets with Pamela Brune, alone. She still loves him and becomes his confessor and Charles is saved from also dying "of fright." He had been madly in love with her, but believed himself to have been rejected. She is now described in terms which in the context are Christian, "the very genius of fortitude, courage winged and inspired and divinely lit."[245]

There are many classic allusions to what may be stages in conversion. After startling him by saying that on the 10th June they will be setting out on their honeymoon, she then begins to help to instil a Christian fortitude in him through a Biblical quotation. Challenging his fatalism with a reminder of Free Will, she says that he must be like Jacob and wrestle with the angel. (*Genesis*, 32:22-32) At first there is doubt that Ottery has the necessary resolve, but proves he "had the grit to go through with it." [246]

The links in the chain continued as even this new crutch is stripped away. He becomes utterly alone for three weeks

---

[242] *Gap*, Ch.VI/II/197-200.
[243] Ibid., Ch.VI/III/203.
[244] Ibid., 204.
[245] Ibid., Ch.VI/IV/210, and Ch.VI/V/213.
[246] Ibid., and Ch.VI/V/212.

when Pamela becomes dangerously ill. Convinced that she will die and soon he will inevitably follow, a great change comes over him one night when he realises that "his life was bereft of every shadow of value" and he was living "in a bleak desert." His fate is no longer important as he centres on her plight. He writes things like "God forgive me." He alludes to Newman's hymn "Lead kindly light." Now entirely alone, there comes upon him ""a wholesale revolution, by which the whole man was moved to a different plane." "Death itself came to have no meaning" when he "discovered the immortality of love. The angel had at last blessed him." All his attempts at salvation by works had failed, and he experienced a conversion through Grace winning that "peace which the world does not give" as "nothing in heaven or earth could harm him now."[247] In this way Buchan echoes the words of Jesus: "Peace I leave with you, my peace I give unto you: not as the world giveth, give I unto you. Let not your heart be troubled, neither let it be afraid." (St John's Gospel, 14:27). Indeed, in losing his life he gained it, and more. (cf. *St Matthew's Gospel*, 16:25[248])

Conversion was for Buchan an intensely private and personal encounter with God, not to be described in detail though the consequences were evident to all who saw the change. The reader is left to work it out for themselves, but the language used shows that Buchan can only mean the transformation in a Christian sense. In his day it was still the Holy Bible, and in general his readers' knowledge of it would have been better than today. He would never have appropriated the words of Jesus about our relationship with the Almighty to describe a human romance. That would have been sacrilege to him and to many of his readers. Wonderful though young love

---

[247] *Gap*, Ch.VI/VI/217-218, for all quotations.
[248] "For whosoever will save his life shall lose it: and whosoever will lose his life for my sake shall find it."

may be it is not really eternal, except in the sense that the Almighty God is eternal. Buchan writes of what "the world does not give." That is "the peace of God" because it "passeth all understanding" and keeps "your hearts and minds through Christ Jesus." (*The Epistle to the Philippians,* 4:7.) Thus the fortitude which Buchan believed in is practised by Ottery, and triumphs because his fortitude, now firmly anchored, overcame his fears. Being Buchan, he can cloak his deepest thoughts in intellectual obscurity (cf. above 142 in Buchan's elegy), but every now and then he comes through with blazing clarity. He does so in *Witch Wood* (1927), and even more so at the last in *Sick Heart River* (1941). For all his tolerance, this is what he really believed about the human condition, and increasingly said so, rather subtly writing, and more overtly in his speeches.

Some readers may think that I have gone too far in my interpretation of the Ottery chapter. Could it be simply that when Charles thinks that both he and Pamela will soon die, he creates a fantasy in which love becomes immortal? They must still explain the Biblical language used, and the Christian hints dropped. Moreover, it is true that Buchan keeps us focused on the human love story, but that still does not explain the extravagance of the language used about immortality which is otherwise out of place.

If we try to get into the mind of Buchan as he was writing, we need to recognise that there was even more Christian significance for someone like him in choosing to include the Jacob story, and the immortality of love. Jacob wrestles with the angel until he is in effect converted. Thereafter he is a changed man. That is how the angel blessed him. Secondly, divine love is especially reflected in human marriage. Portrayed as echoing the love affair between Christ and His Church, it is the Bride of Christ (*Second Corinthians,* 11:2, & *Ephesians* 5, 21-24). In one with Buchan's upbringing, and strong personal commitment to the faith, it was natural, sometimes even subconsciously, for him to use such Biblical illustrations in his writing. These allusions clinch the argument that he was here engaged in commending the Christian message. He was, after all, a noted wartime propagandist, and is now adapting the same technique in the spiritual conflict in which he believed himself to be engaged. That is evident from reading the last three pages of *Memory-Hold-the-Door*.

With him, fortitude is the ability consistently to face dire threats to one's well-being by the constant belief in something positive which is greater than one's fears. He had this for himself in his experience of Christ, and commends the same through Ottery. Alastair had it too. Similarly supported, his fortitude enabled him to cope with the miseries of war, as Ottery did over his awful foreknowledge. Indeed, we have seen how habitually Alastair was thought to have achieved this through his steadfast humour and encouragement of others. He could do this because he had found the same rock as his brothers. Others might discover fortitude elsewhere, but the Christian faith was Buchan's chosen method, and the one he recommended.

Notes with the Postscript

1. Polygon references: There are various editions and printings of *The Gap in the Curtain*. Pages numbers are usually cited in the First Edition which may not be readily available. In the hope of assisting the reader, the more recent and easily accessible Polygon edition is then quoted, giving the Chapter in Roman numerals, followed by the section, and then the page number. An equally apposite practice is adopted with *The Dancing Floor*, see above 128, 129.

2. Buchan's descriptions of Conversion: In the short story, "Space" (written in 1910), Buchan had used the same method, as with Ottery, of quoting a hauntingly familiar Biblical text followed later by a radical change in one of his characters. Hollond is exploring the unseen space around us and there encounters objects and people. As a scientist trying to grasp the meaning of this, he goes through

disturbing experiences. In the end he takes the train to Switzerland unnerved, feeling "on the edge of a terror." He is not a man of faith but before he is killed, solitarily climbing in the Alps, he sends Leithen an enigmatic postcard saying, "*I know at last – God's mercy. – H.G.H.*" Readers are left to make of this what they will, though Buchan hints at some kind of conversion experience, with Leithen saying that Hollond "had gone so far into the land of pure spirit that he must needs go further and shed the fleshly envelope that encumbered him" and curiously adding "God send that he found rest!" The suggestion is that he deliberately wanted to fall to his death. Twenty years later (1932) Buchan is much more explicit in describing the change in Ottery. That is consistent with what I have described elsewhere as the curve in his thinking about the essential nature of Christianity. He moved from his youthful evangelical world to a more liberal view, and as a result of the War back towards a more evangelical belief which stressed the need for conversion.

Endnote: Why was "O. Douglas" Anna Buchan's Pseudonym?
(carried over from page 6 above)

Anna played a very large role in Alastair's upbringing. We have seen that she was responsible for preserving much of the detail that we know about him. Some readers may have been puzzled over her choice of "O. Douglas" for a pseudonym. Her first novel, *Olivia in India* (1913), is written in the first person by an Olivia Douglas. Apparently she adopted that identity to conceal her own, not wishing to tarnish her brother's growing reputation with the yet unknown reception to her first novel but having become well-known, kept on using it. She could have gained publicity from advertising herself as Buchan's brother, but his widow tells of 'her fastidious reserve" being "the very soul of reticence."[249] With her love of Shakespeare, Lownie tells us that Olivia is taken from *Twelfth Night*. He is probably right because Anna's niece recalls that she soon became not

---

[249] Tweedsmuir, S. in Buchan, A., *Farewell to Priorsford*, 25 & 40.

"Aunt" but remained "the Olivia of such dear memory" She adds that "I can hear you quoting the speech from Twelfth Night that ends with [the] line

> *...and make the babbling gossip of the air*
> *Cry out 'Olivia'!*

and your soft Scotch voice dwelling on the name."[250]

As for Douglas, it was a noted Border surname. I can find no obvious family or friendly connection between the two families. Ursula Buchan has commented to me that the hero of some of the stories told to the Buchan children by their father was Sir James Douglas, the lieutenant to Robert the Bruce. He

40. Detail from William Hole's Frieze

became known to the Scots as the "Good Sir James", but to the English as the "Black Douglas", for good reason. In their strongly partisan Scottish way which led to their snubbing of an English cousin,[251] Douglas was a hero to them as children.

Perhaps a memory of the Buchan-Douglas link stayed

---

[250] Fairfax-Lucy, A., in Buchan, A., *Farewell to Priorsford*, 49.
[251] Buchan, A., *Unforgettable*, 14.

with her after their childish appropriations from heroic Scottish history into their own family fable.

It intrigues me that later Anna was very familiar with Edinburgh, and must have seen William Hole's frieze in the entrance hall of the Scottish National Portrait Gallery in that city. It depicts the leaders of Scottish Independence.

The Countess of Buchan, who crowned Robert the Bruce (see above, 150), stands behind his left shoulder, with Douglas at his right hand. The two names are printed boldly above on each side of the Bruce. Anna must have known of this work as it was greatly acclaimed when it was finished in 1898. She may have noticed the linked names and kept them in mind so that they remained with her, perhaps unconsciously. Could either, or more likely both, have been her inspiration? Some will find this fanciful, or just a bit of fun, but that does not deny the fact that these names were closely linked in what they were taught about heroic Scottish history at their father's knee. Anyway, it satisfies my own conceit to have discovered the names so linked together, and I have not found that anyone has put forward another explanation. It was a surname that she used for her mother later in her fiction.

Endnote: *Farewell to Priorsford*

Anna and her siblings were exceptionally able. Like Buchan, in her own way Anna was a very successful novelist. William would probably have become the Governor of an Indian Province, or reached some other eminence. Walter had been destined for the Scottish Bar, where he might have become a Scottish high court judge as a Senator of the College of Justice. Alastair, all unfulfilled, we have considered.

Anna Buchan (1877-1948) was Alastair's older sister. Her name is attached to *Farewell to Priorsford,* which was published two years after her death. It is sometimes described as her autobiography, but it is not. Rather, it is an *in memoriam* composed of five articles about her by relatives and friends, and five of her own stories. The title is significant because she had previously written a novel called *Priorsford* (1932), which was her fictional name for Peebles.[252] It can be misleading that, coming out two years after her death, the sub-title is "by and about Anna Buchan", and the dust jacket proclaims, "And Farewell to 'O. Douglas'". Living in this Royal Burgh for the last forty years of her life, she had become a famous resident and, like Buchan, had been given the Freedom, and made Warden of Neidpath Castle nearby. Unlike her earlier books of memoirs which concerned the family more than herself, it adds nothing about Alastair who had a crucial share in a decade of the lives of Anna and her brother, Walter. In it he receives only cursory mentions by others, nothing directly by her. Even in *Unforgettable, Unforgotten* (1945) Anna tends to repeat what she had said earlier in her book in his memory. Such repetition is something that Buchan also did a little in books and more often in speeches. Indeed, in so doing both were addressing different, or wider audiences, when they borrowed from past work and thus made it legitimate to do so. *Farewell to Priorsford* is mentioned here to satisfy the curiosity of any enquiring reader who may question why it has otherwise been omitted, and suppose that other published details about Alastair may have been neglected.

Nevertheless, I have learnt much from returning to this book. Most was gleaned from A. G. Reekie's 'Biographical Introduction' and from Susan Tweedsmuir. No clue was given to Reekie's identity but I found three books under such a name. The title of one being *The Way to Worship* suggested that he might have been an ordained minister. Obviously a close friend of Anna, Arthur Glendinning Reekie (1905-1951), turned out to have been an evangelical clergyman who had been ordained

---

[252] Reekie, "Biographical Introduction", 11.

into the Scottish Congregational Church in Glasgow in 1930, and served there for thirteen years. There is an easily explained two year gap in his ministry from 1943-1945. Already ill, his home in Clydebank was totally destroyed by enemy action in the Blitz of 1943. It seems likely that his health never recovered from this double affliction and, after this long gap, he accepted the small pastorate at Walkerburn Congregation Church, eight miles from Peebles.[253] He loved being in the countryside and it gave him opportunity to develop his writing.

It is not clear how he came to know Anna so well and it seems surprising. He only arrived in the Borders in 1945. Within three years she was dead. His previous life and ministry had been in Edinburgh and Glasgow. She won't have been in his Walkerburn congregation, so they probably met through intellectual and Christian circles in Peebles, the nearby town. The reason for their mutual understanding is more obvious. He is described as "a man of catholic interest", with a "wide knowledge of literature, drama, and music, together with [a] deep understanding of humanity." He may have known Anna only in the last years of her life but still displays an intimate knowledge of her, so much so that he was asked by the family to write this appreciation. That is sufficient testimony to his suitability even if he had known her only during her last few years. Though a much younger happily married man, he shared some of the characteristics of her father as well as his theology. He was a good choice for the "Introduction" being himself both an author and one who had also published scholarly papers. In addition he contributed many articles to the *British Weekly* and *Evening Dispatch*. In 1947 he became editor of *The Scottish Congregationalist*. At the time of his death he had resigned from his ministry wishing "to be free for a time from pastoral

---

[253] Entry in McNaughton. Other details are gleaned from *The Scottish Congregationalist.*

duties" and had just begun the Church and People series under the pen-name "Matthew Mark". He often wrote under other pseudonyms like "Mungo Dunedin" and "Paul Parson".

His vivid portrait of Anna reveals how successful the Reverend Mr Buchan was as a father, and how much she owed to him. She came from a deeply close knit family as has often been recorded.[254] In it there

> was a reverence for the gift of imagination. The children grew up in a fellowship in which they were held together by the most powerful bonds. Their family circle was a magic circle; their home a secret order of delight and its shrines were religion and literature. To the Reverend John Buchan and his wife was given the knowledge of how to raise a family so that all the talent within it was allowed to grow and flourish.[255]

We shall see that they gained more than this from their father, and there was not a dud or a rebel among these siblings.

Throughout the lives of these children they remained closely in touch and deeply concerned about each other. It was different in Mr Buchan's own generation. Two of his three brothers lived rather estranged from the rest of the family. Alexander left Scotland and lived in Hampshire, having something to do with English law there, though I have not found him in the *Law List* as a barrister or solicitor. He was the first to die, shortly before Willie. In writing of his clerical grandfather, the 3rd Baron seems unaware of Alexander's existence.[256] Then, there was Tom, the rolling stone who became "religious" in his later years. The two sisters were apparently blameless, amicably retiring to Guernsey to let the

---

[254] The sense of this long out-lived him as the 3rd Baron tells us, Buchan, W. *John Buchan*, 172.
[255] Reekie, "Biographical Introduction", 16
[256] Buchan W., *John Buchan*, 62-63. "My great-grandfather had 3 sons."

next generation into Bank House. All except Mr Buchan were unmarried.

Reekie testifies that like her father Anna possessed an exemplary trait of generosity in giving to others. Indeed, her mother had it too, as well as Buchan and the other siblings. Susan said that before she knew Anna, she "met many kind and generous people, but I had never before come in contact with any one family who economised so much on themselves and gave away money so unsparingly."[257]

Secondly, she was good with people, being a skilled and readily sympathetic listener.[258] People felt that they mattered. Mr Buchan was the same, as was Buchan, William in India, and Alastair with his men.

The Christian faith, as taught by her father, was Anna's bedrock. What Reekie wrote was read, and was approved for publication by those who were closest to Anna within her own family.

> Though her love for her mother was obvious to all, her father's teaching [and example, see below] had reached the deep heart's core. The intense evangelical faith of the Reverend John Buchan had quickened no one more than his own daughter. She was his best disciple; for the inspiration of her life she drew deeply from his saintly example.... To Anna her father was another Mr Standfast, and only she could have told all that he counted for in every day of her life.[259]

I have shown that it was so with Buchan and now with Alastair. Ursula Buchan has done the same with William. Walter is perhaps the dark horse about whom far less has been written. I do not put much credence on the 3rd Baron's scepticism about

---

[257] Buchan, A. *Farewell*, 45
[258] Reekie, "Biographical Introduction", 32
[259] Ibid., 24 – see also 38.

how little depth he thought there was perhaps in Uncle Willie's faith.[260] Especially in those days, the fact that he was pressed to become an Elder shows that he was thought worthy to mentor other Christians. Walter may have felt the same constraints because he held the same public offices in a small community.

Moreover, all the Buchans had a natural modesty and reserve, which is why it can be hard to chance upon the clues about their Christianity, but they are there. Reekie is the first to have really opened my eyes about Anna, and Walter has not had so revealing a biographer.[261] Among themselves the common faith of his brother's children was known, accepted and did not need to be spoken. It probably took an outsider like Reekie with Anna, the missionaries in India with William, and the Chaplain with Alastair, to make their Christian faith so explicitly known. Walter was very close to both Anna and their brother John, and we have seen him share their Christian reaction to Alastair's death. This generation of Buchans all lived honourable lives in concord with the true spirit of their father's teaching, and the family motto:

Non inferiora secutus

I am much indebted to Tracey Wilson of the National Library of Scotland for generous assistance in obtaining information about A. G. Reekie which was inaccessible to me because of the Covid-19 lockdown. This went beyond the call of duty.

---

[260] Buchan, W., *John Buchan*, 64-65; for Uncle Willie's faith see Weekes, *John Buchan's Faith*, 112-116.
[261] Sheila Scott, in her brief booklet, *J. Walter Buchan*, 3 only reports appreciative comments about him as a young man teaching in the Sabbath School in his father's church and his interest in Young Men's Associations. She does not make us fell that "one of the pleasures of a visit to Bank House was a brief sight of that brisk and twinkling man." Buchan, W. *John Buchan*, 171.

Addendum

Forrester, Wendy. *Anna Buchan and O. Douglas*. London: Maitland Press, 1995.

Anna was such a crucial influence in Alastair's upbringing so that her character is important here. This book came to hand after I had written about O. Douglas (above, 196-197). Forrester agrees that the pen name was adapted from the heroine of *Olivia in India*, but does not say why that character's name was chosen (40). I have gone a little deeper. About her Christian faith (cf. above, 202) she said this:

> Anna was generally reticent about religion, and embarrassed by those with a more outspoken attitude, but she expresses her faith sincerely, though briefly, when Olivia argues with her lover about "the darkness of what comes after. How can it be dark when the Sun of Righteousness has arisen?…this I know, that if we hold fast to the substance of things hoped for, the evidence of things not seen, looking to Jesus, the author and finisher of our faith, then, when the end comes, we shall be able to lay our heads down like children saying, this night when I lie down to sleep, in sure and certain hope that when, having done with houses made by hands, we wake in the House of Many Mansions, it will be what John Bunyan calls a 'sunshine morning'." (46)[262]

"Her books…were romances…founded on a bedrock of sober sense and religious faith." (7

---

[262] Like Buchan, Anna is saturated in the Scriptures and quotes them naturally. "Sun of Righteousness" comes from *Malachi*, 4:2; "the author and finisher of our faith" from *Hebrews*, 12:2; "The substance of things hoped for, the evidence of things not seen" from *Hebrews* 11:1; "sure and certain hope" from The Book of Common Prayer and based on passages like "the many mansions" from *St John's Gospel*, 14:2.

Bibliography

Archives

The Gordon Highlanders Museum, Aberdeen.

The Hutchesons' Educational Trust Archive, Glasgow.

The Imperial War Museum, London.

The John Buchan Story, a John Buchan Society resource at Peebles.

The National Archives, Kew.

The National Archives of Scotland, Edinburgh.

The National Library of Scotland, Special Collections, Edinburgh.

Pembroke College, Cambridge, Archive.

The Royal Scots Museum, Edinburgh Castle.

The University of Glasgow Archive.

Books Quoted and Consulted

Adam Smith, Janet. *John Buchan.* London: Rupert Hart-Davis, 1965.

Army Lists, 1915 and 1916.

Arnander, Christopher (ed.). *Private Lord Crawford's Great War Diaries: From Medical Orderly to Cabinet Minister.* Barnsley: Pen and Sword, 2014.

Baring, Maurice. "To Julian Grenfell": various editions.

Beith, John H. Pseud. "Ian Hay". *The First Hundred Thousand.* Edinburgh: William Blackwood, 1915.

British Library, Asian and African Collection IOR/2/AG/34/29/158, 39-40 and 104-105.

Brooke, Rupert. "The Dead": various editions.

Bryce, Mary R. L. *John Veitch a Memoir.* Edinburgh: W. Blackwood & Sons, 1896.

Buchan, A. E. "Officer's Record". National Archives, Kew, WO 339/26528.

Buchan, Alastair. Papers in the National Library of Scotland (hereafter NLS) Acc. 11627/37.

Buchan, Alastair. Vandyk, "Photograph" in NLS 11627/76a.

Buchan, Anna. et al. *Alastair Buchan 1894-1917.* Peebles: privately printed, 1917.

Buchan, Anna, (Douglas, O. pseud.). *Ann and her Mother*. London: Nelson, 1922.

Buchan, Anna, *Farewell to Priorsford*. London: Hodder & Stoughton, 1950.

Buchan, Anna, (Douglas, O. pseud.). *The Setons*. London: Hodder and Stoughton, 1917.

Buchan, Anna. *Unforgettable, Unforgotten*. London: Hodder & Stoughton, 1945.

Buchan, John. *The Blanket of the Dark*. London: Hodder and Stoughton, 1931.

Buchan, John. *The Causal and the Casual in History*. Cambridge: Cambridge University Press, 1929.

Buchan, John. "The Company of the Marjolaine" in Lownie, Andrew, *John Buchan: The Complete Short Stories, Volume III*. London: Thistle, 1997.

Buchan, John. *The Dancing Floor*. London: Hodder and Stoughton, 1925. Polygon edition, Edinburgh: Birlinn, 2012.

Buchan, John. *The Gap in the Curtain*. London: Hodder & Stoughton, 1932; Polygon edition, Edinburgh: Birlinn, 2012.

Buchan, John. *Francis and Riversdale Grenfell*. London: Thomas Nelson, 1919.

Buchan, John. *The History of the Royal Scots Fusiliers.* London: Thomas Nelson, 1925.

Buchan, John. *The Island of Sheep.* London: Hodder and Stoughton, 1936.

Buchan, John. *The Long Road to Victory.* London: Thomas Nelson and Son, 1920.

Buchan, John. *The Magic Walking Stick.* London: Hodder and Stoughton, 1932.

Buchan, John. *Memory-Hold-the-Door.* London: Hodder and Stoughton, 1940.

Buchan, John. *Mr Standfast.* London: Hodder & Stoughton, 1919; Polygon edition, Edinburgh: Birlinn, 2014

Buchan, John. *Oliver Cromwell.* London: Hodder & Stoughton, 1934.

Buchan, John. *Presbyterianism Yesterday, Today, and Tomorrow.* Edinburgh: Church of Scotland, 1938.

Buchan, John. *Sick Heart River.* London: Hodder and Stoughton, 1941.

Buchan, John. *Witch Wood.* London: Hodder and Stoughton, 1927.

Buchan, John with Stewart, John. *The Fifteenth (Scottish) Division 1914-1919.* Edinburgh: Wm. Blackwood & Sons, 1926.

Buchan, Susan (see Lady Tweedsmuir).

Buchan, Ursula. *Beyond the Thirty-Nine Steps.* London: Bloomsbury, 2019.

Buchan, Ursula. "W.H.B." *John Buchan Journal*, 52 (2019), 10-20.

Buchan, William. *John Buchan a Memoir.* London: Buchan and Enright, 1982.

Buckingham, Ian. "Tweeddale History – the Family." *Peeblesshire News*, 23rd April 2017.

Bullock, John M. & Constance O. Skelton. *A Notable Military Family: The Gordons of Griamachary in the Parish of Kildonan* (Arran). Huntly: Ross-shire Printing and Publishing (J. Dunbar), 1907.

Burke's Landed Gentry. London: Burke's Peerage Ltd, 1939.

Burke's Landed Gentry of Great Britain: The Kingdom of Scotland, Vol. 1. Stokesley: Burke's Peerage and Gentry, 2001.

Carswell, Catherine. "A Perspective", in Tweedsmuir, Lady, *John Buchan by his Wife and Friends*, 148-173.

Cecil, Hugh. "The Diary that proves Anthony Seldon wrong about the First World War and the Public Schools", *The Spectator*, 12th April 2014.

Commonwealth War Graves Commission website "Find a Grave".

Cowan, John. *Canada's Governors-General*. Toronto: York Publishing Co., 1965.

Ewing, John. *The Royal Scots 1914-1919*. Edinburgh: Oliver and Boyd, 1925.

Fairlie, Henry. *The Kennedy Promise*. London: Doubleday, 1973.

Forsyth, David & Ugolini, Wendy. *A Global Force*. Edinburgh: Edinburgh University Press, 2017. (Hyslop, Jonathan. "South Africa and Scotland in the First World War", included as Ch.7, 150-167.)

Gibb, Andrew Dewar. *With Winston Churchill at the Front*. Barnsley: Frontline Books, 2016.

Gibbon, Lewis Grassic. *Sunset Song*. Edinburgh: Polygon, 2015.

Gilbert, Martin. *Winston S. Churchill, Vol.III 1914-1916*. London: Heinemann, 1971.

Gilbert, Martin. *Churchill: A Life*. London: Pimlico, 2000.

Golin, Malcolm. "John Buchan's Heraldry, his Peerage and Honours". *John Buchan Journal*, 25 (Autumn 2001), 26-37.

Greig, James C. G. "In Journeyings Often…." *John Buchan Journal*, 11 (Spring 1992), 15-17.

Gunn, Clement B. *The Book of Remembrance for Tweeddale, Book 1, Burgh and Parish of Peebles*. 1920. Neidpath Press, 1920.

Hastings, Max. *Catastrophe 1914: Europe Goes to War*. New York: 2013.

Hay, Ian, see Beith, J. H.

Hillier, Kenneth (Ed.). *The First Editions of John Buchan*. North Somerset: Avonworld, 2008.

Hyslop, Jonathan, see Forsyth.

Innes of Learney, Sir Thomas. *Scots Heraldry*. Edinburgh: Oliver and Boyd, 1934.

Kilmuir, Earl of (David Maxwell Fyfe). *Political Adventure: Memoirs*. London: Weidenfeld and Nicholson, 1964.

Lang, (Sir) Peter Redford Scott. *Roll of Honour and Roll of Service, 1914-1919, University of St Andrews*. Edinburgh: R & R Clark, 1920.

Lee, Edwin R. "Thomas Henderson Buchan", *John Buchan Journal*, 21 (Autumn 1999), 2-13.

Lee, Edwin R. "Buchan and Christian Platonism", *John Buchan Journal*, 38 (Autumn 2008), 2-13.

Lindsay, Samuel. *Coatbridge and the Great War*. Glasgow: Hay Nisbet, 1919.

Lownie, Andrew. *John Buchan: The Presbyterian Cavalier*. London: Pimlico, 1995

Lownie, Andrew. *John Buchan: The Complete Short Stories, Volume III*. London: Thistle, 1997.

Lownie, Andrew, and Milne, W. *John Buchan's Collected Poems*. Aberdeen: Scottish Cultural Press, 1996.

Macdonald, Kate. *John Buchan A Companion to the Mystery Fiction*. Jefferson, NC: McFarland, 2008.

McNaughton, William D. *The Scottish Congregational Ministry 1794-1993*. Glasgow: The Congregational Union of Scotland, 1993.

Malden, John and Eilean. "An Heraldic Hierarchy." *The Double Treasure*, 16 (1994); The Heraldry Society of Scotland.

Osborn, Edward B. *The Muse in Arms*. London: John Murray, 1917.

Oxford Dictionary of National Biography.

Pembroke College Annual Gazette, 1918. Cambridge: Pembroke College Archive.

Pilditch, Jan. *Catherine Carswell: a biography*. Edinburgh: John Donald, 2007.

Pilditch, Jan (Ed.). *Selected Letters of Catherine Carswell*. Edinburgh: Kennedy and Boyd, 2016.

Reitz, D. *Adrift on the Open Veldt*. Capetown: Stomberg, 1999. (Republished in *Trekking On*.)

Royal Scots Fusiliers Magazine, 1918.

St Columba's Magazine [Pont Street], March 1940.

Scott, Sheila, *J. Walter Buchan*. Selkirk: printed by Walter Thomson at the *Advertiser* Office, 1993.

Scott-Giles, Charles. W. *Boutell's Heraldry*. London: Frederick Warne, 1950

Skeil, Alexander P. "Officer's Record". National Archives, Kew, WO 339/37170.

Skeil, Alexander, P. "The River Column in North Russia August 1918-July 1919" in Buchan, John, *The Long Road to Victory*. London: Thomas Nelson and Son, 1920, 297-332.

Smith, Janet Adam. *John Buchan*. London: Rupert Hart-Davis, 1965.

Smith, Thomas "Officer's Record". National Archives, Kew, WO 339/12071.

Soames, Mary. *Speaking for Themselves*. London: Doubleday, 1998.

Sorley, Charles H. "To Germany". In Osborn, E. B., *The Muse in Arms*. London: John Murray, 1917.

Stewart, John, and Buchan, John. *The Fifteenth (Scottish Division 1914-1919)*. Edinburgh: Wm. Blackwood & Sons, 1926.

Strachan, Hew. 'Introduction" to Buchan, John. *Mr Standfast*. Polygon edition, Edinburgh: Birlinn, 2014

Thomas, D. "France 1992", *John Buchan Journal* 12 (Autumn 1992), 12-16.

Tweedsmuir, Susan (Lady). *John Buchan by his Wife and Friends.* London: Hodder & Stoughton, 1947.

University of Glasgow Calendar 1915-16.

"University of Glasgow Story" online.

"War Diary of the 6th Royal Scots Fusiliers". The National Archives, Kew: WO 95/1772/3.

"War Diary of the 6/7th Royal Scots Fusiliers". The National Archives, Kew: WO 95/1947/2.

Weekes, David. "Lieutenant Alastair Buchan, R.S.F." *John Buchan Journal* 52 (2019), 21-28.

Weekes, David. *John Buchan, 1875-1940 (First Baron Tweedsmuir of Elsfield....),* see v, above.

Weekes, David. *John Buchan's Faith Experienced in His Life.* London: Lavender Inprint, 2022.

Wellington College Register 1859-1896. Wellington College, 1898.

Who Was Who. London: A & C Black, various volumes by date.

Winterbotham, Cyril W. "The Cross of Wood". In Osborn, E. B., *The Muse in Arms.* London: John Murray, 1917.

Wordsworth, William. "The Character of the Happy Warrior", 1806.

Wright, Damien. *Churchill's Secret War with Lenin*. Solihull: Helion, 2017.

Newspapers and Journals

Berwickshire News, 11th September 1951, 7 "Died in Hospital" (A. G. Reekie).

Church Times, 1st September 2017, "He who would true valour see".

Coatbridge Advertiser, 6th October 1923, "Skeil's Cricket".

Coatbridge Express, 18th April 1917, "Skeil, Wounded" and 26th September 1934, "Skeil, Chairman of the British Legion".

Coatbridge Leader, 8th August 1925, "Skeil's Marriage".

Glasgow Evening Times, "Roll of Honour January-April 1917".

Glasgow Herald, 11th February 1959, "Skeil's Funeral Intimation".

Illustrated London News, 27th February 1917, Smith "Roll of Honour".

London Gazette, 24th November 1914, "Stevenson, commissioned" and 3rd January 1917, "Buchan, promoted Lieutenant".

Peeblesshire News, 23rd April 2017, "Tweeddale's History – the Buchan Family".

The National, 5th November 2018, "'They Died for a World that is Past': The First World War Remembered."

The Spectator, 12th April 2014, Cecil on "Crawford's War Diaries".

The Times, 10th April 2020, "Boyhood Tales of Valour Came True for Double VC".

The Times Literary Supplement, 3rd May 1917, "The Soldier Patriot".

Wishaw Press. 4th July 1947, "Retiral of Newmains Headmaster".

INDEX

Though every effort has been made to be consistent, some references may be a page either side of those quoted.

Printed in Great Britain
by Amazon

11082806R00149